SO YOU THINK YOU KNOW THE LORD OF THE RINGS?

Clive Gifford

a division of Hodder Headline Limited

© Copyright Hodder & Stoughton Ltd 2002

Published in Great Britain in 2002
by Hodder Children's Books

Editor: Isabel Thurston
Design by Fiona Webb
Cover design: Hodder Children's Books

10 9 8 7 6 5

ISBN: 0340873612

Printed by Bookmarque Ltd, Croydon, Surrey

The paper and board used in this paperback by Hodder Children's Books are natural recyclable products made from wood grown in sustainable forests. The manufacturing processes conform to the environmental regulations of the country of origin.

Hodder Children's Books
a division of Hodder Headline Limited
338 Euston Road
London NW1 3BH

Contents

Introduction

So you think you know all about Middle-earth and the epic quest undertaken by Frodo, Sam and the Company of the Ring to defeat the dark forces of Mordor?

J.R.R. Tolkien's incredible tale of power, courage, friendship and evil has captivated millions of people ever since it was first published in 1954. This quiz book is designed to test to the full your knowledge of the extraordinary array of people, places and events which make up the strange and fabulous world of **The Lord of the Rings**.

There are 1200 questions in all: 450 about The Fellowship of the Ring, 400 about The Two Towers and 350 about The Return of the King. Some you may find as simple as hobbits find feasting. Others may taunt you as much as the Ring did Gollum. But don't be tempted to turn to the back for the answers until you've completed a section of questions.

Good luck!

Questions about The Fellowship of the Ring

1. What colour is Gandalf's long hair?

2. What is the surname of the hobbit called Bilbo?

3. Is the Prancing Pony inn a one-storey, two-storey, three-storey or four-storey building?

4. Is Rivendell north, south, east or west from Hobbiton?

5. Who calls herself 'daughter of the River'?

6. How many weeks does Strider tell the hobbits it will take them to travel from Weathertop to Rivendell?

7. Who hacked the tentacles away from Frodo?

8. What did Mr Maggot mainly grow on his farm?

9. Hobbits' favourite colours for clothing are: green and yellow, red and pink or blue and black?

10. Who gave those setting out from Rivendell the group name of the Company of the Ring?

11. Black Riders use their horses to see for them: true or false?

12. According to the elven-lore verse, how many rings are there for the Elven-kings?

13. Gimli is the son of a dwarf; what was the name of his father?

14. What happened to the hobbits' ponies after the night spent at the Prancing Pony inn?

15. To whom did Lady Galadriel give a small crystal phial as a present?

16. What sort of creatures are Nob and Bob?

17. What is the surname of the hobbits Odo and Sancho: Proudfoot, Bolger or Brandybuck?

18. Is Fangorn a mountain, a forest, a river or a marsh?

19. Is Gandalf an elf, dwarf, orc or wizard?

20. What sort of creature rescued Gandalf from Saruman's clutches?

21. What does Frodo put on to escape the attack of Boromir?

22. Is Nimrodel a stream, mountain, cave system or lake?

23. What was the name of the healing plant Strider used on Frodo's wound?

24. Is Merry Brandybuck, Merry Bolger or Merry Brandywine, one of Frodo's closest friends?

25. Who forgot to send Frodo a letter from Gandalf?

26. By what method of transport did Frodo attempt to leave the Company of the Ring?

27. Of the ten dwarves who survived the Battle of Five Armies, how many still lived in the Dwarf-kingdom?

28. Lúthien rescued Beren from which evil person's dungeons?

29. How many times had Gildor seen Bilbo Baggins since he left Bag End?

30. What are Harfoots and Stoors?

31. Who drove Frodo, Pippin and Sam to the ferry over the Brandywine?

32. Was the King of the Dwarves over 50, over 150 or over 250 years old?

33. Which hobbit travelled by pony from Weathertop onwards?

34. Which man accompanied Lady Galadriel in the Swan-ship on the Silverlode river?

35. The Black Riders are: ringwraiths, fallen wizards, trolls or banshees?

36. Milo Burrows never answered letters: what golden present did Bilbo leave for him?

37. Who declares at the Council of Elrond that he will head to Minas Tirith?

38. Which hobbit received two sacks of potatoes, a spade, ointment and a waistcoat from Bilbo?

39. Which of the three hobbits did Farmer Maggot's dogs ignore?

40. Which hobbit worked out where Frodo was even though he was invisible?

41. Which member of Frodo's party chose not to mix with the guests at the Prancing Pony inn?

42. What river flows out of the Downs and through the Old Forest?

43. Who starts a fire by using a magic chant to help melt the snow from around the Company?

44. Bilbo left Hugo Bracegirdle an overcoat, an empty bookcase or a mirror?

45. What was used to power and steer the boats that the Company travelled in?

46. Which type of hobbit was most friendly with elves: Stoors, Harfoots or Fallohides?

47. Uruks of Mordor are: trolls, wolves, orcs or crows?

48. Who rescued Frodo from being drowned by the River Withywindle?

49. Does Frodo tell those at the Prancing Pony inn that he is searching for treasure, looking for Gandalf or writing a book?

50. What item lay across the necks of Pippin, Sam and Merry in the barrow?

QUIZ 2

1. Who, along with Gandalf, tried to track Gollum through the Wilderland?

2. What did Gollum use to float on the Great River?

3. What is Gildor the elf's surname: Intrepida, Inglorion or Interruptum?

4. Which of the following were **not** names of the hobbits' ponies: Sharp-ears, Wise-nose, Flick-tail or White-socks?

5. What is the name of the chief town of the Shire?

6. Who killed the first wolf to attack the Company?

7. What device helped Frodo to climb into the trees of Golden Wood?

8. What colour was the elf-stone, called a beryl, that Strider found near the Last Bridge?

9. Which one of the following dwarves was not still living in the Dwarf-kingdom: Bifur, Ori, Bofur or Bombur?

10. Caradhras is a stream, mountain, lake or citadel?

11. Were the Farthings named after planets, the seasons or the points of the compass?

12. Which bird in large flocks forced the Company of the Ring to put out their fire?

13. Whose tomb was found in the Chamber of Mazarbul?

14. Which two hobbits did Boromir carry through the snow?

15. How many arches does the Last Bridge have: one, two, three or four?

16. Who lived in earlier times at Dol Guldur: Elrond, the Dark Lord, Bilbo or Glóin?

17. How long does Frodo ask for to make the decision to go west to Gondor or east to the Fear and Shadow?

18. What sort of weapon, called Sting, did Bilbo hang over his fireplace?

19. Which one of these settlements was not found in Bree-land: Combe, Staddle or Waymoot?

20. The Horn-call of Buckland has not been sounded for how many years: 20, 40 or 100?

21. Who does Frodo first see when waking up in Rivendell?

22. Which member of the Company of the Ring comes from Minas Tirith?

23. Which council drove the evil power out of Mirkwood?

24. Sirannon, the Gate-stream, had been dammed to create what geographical feature?

25. How many nights did Frodo lie asleep at Rivendell?

26. Who started out in the boat with Sam and Aragorn?

27. How many ponies did the hobbits leave the village of Bree with?

28. By what name did the people of Bree call the mysterious tall, dark wanderers?

29. What was the double-barrelled surname of Bilbo's unpleasant relatives, Otho and Lobelia?

30. What happened to Frodo's sword when the leader of the Black Riders held out his hand?

31. What is the name of the two stone pillars on the banks of the Great River?

32. Which two members of the Baggins family have the same birthday?

33. Bilbo left a case of silver spoons to which of his female relatives?

34. What gift given by Lady Galadriel to the Company shines light in the dark?

35. What does Gandalf call the ring that is in Frodo's possession?

36. What place does Sam see when he stares into the Mirror of Galadriel?

37. How many years was it since Bilbo had returned to the Shires with his treasure?

38. Which wizard lives in Isengard?

39. What sort of building was once on top of Weathertop hill?

40. How many meals a day is the ideal number for a hobbit?

41. What is the name of the pub with the best beer in the Eastfarthing?

42. Who, beginning with the letter G, was the last of the great Elf-kings of Middle-earth?

43. Did Frodo set out on his quest from Bag End on foot, on a pony, in a boat or by car?

44. Into what hall do the guests head after Frodo's first feast at Rivendell?

45. How many breeds of hobbit were there originally: one, three or eleven?

46. What is Gandalf's full name?

47. In what area, beginning with the letter C, did Frodo buy a house?

48. What was the food in the basket Mrs Maggot left for the Hobbits?

49. The Greenway is a grassed-over road found in Bree-land, the Westfarthing or Buckland?

50. Which two hobbits received silver belts from Lady Galadriel?

QUIZ 3

1. What colour was the horse Glorfindel rode?

2. Who volunteers at the Council of Elrond to take the ring to the Mountain of Fire?

3. Balin was lord of Moria: true or false?

4. What was Ham Gamgee's nickname: Mr Greenfingers, Gardening Gamgee or the Gaffer?

5. What facial feature did no Fallohide or Harfoot hobbit have?

6. What item of Gandalf's breaks when he damages the bridge in Moria?

7. Which hobbit is writing a book about his adventures?

8. Just before reaching which ford were the hobbits set upon by all nine Black Riders?

9. What was the name, beginning with the letter H, of the gatekeeper at the Greenway?

10. What hall did Gorhendad Oldbuck build?

11. Who referred to the ring as his 'precious'?

12. Which of the following surnames was not present at Bilbo's party: Brandybuck, Tobleycold, Proudfoot or Hornblower?

13. Who does Gandalf order to leave Bag End with Frodo on his quest?

14. How many nights do the hobbits spend at Tom Bombadil's house?

15. What is Strider's true name?

16. What metal did the magic ring in Bilbo's care appeared to be made of?

17. Lady Galadriel and her maidens wove the clothes given to the Company of the Ring at Rivendell: true or false?

18. In his letter to Frodo, what does Gandalf say about travelling at night?

19. Which farmer is Frodo scared of after being caught stealing when he was young?

20. What place, beginning with the letter R, does Frodo head for on leaving Bag End?

21. What is the first group of non-hobbit creatures Frodo, Sam and Pippin encounter on their journey?

22. The Dark Lord made the ring in Frodo's possession: true or false?

23. What item did each of the hobbits take from the treasure in the barrow?

24. Who represented the dwarves in the Company of the Ring?

25. What is the name of the dwarf who Frodo first talks to at Rivendell?

26. What did the Big Folk of Bree-land call the hobbits who lived there?

27. By what other name did Sméagol become known?

28. What is the name in English of the most desired material in Middle-earth?

29. In which mountain were the rings forged?

30. Amun Sûl is an ancient tower, village, palace or leader of dwarves?

31. What did Gorhendad Oldbuck change his surname to?

32. Was the Mayor of Michel Delving elected every two, three or seven years?

33. Which one of Frodo's friends admits he has known about the ring for many years?

34. In Gondor, what sort of building's name started with the word Minas?

35. The Cracks of Doom are found in a desert, a mountain or at the bottom of a lake?

36. What creatures cut down and burned hundreds of trees in the Old Forest?

37. What part of Frodo's body was injured by Black Riders at Weathertop?

38. Lady Galadriel summoned the White Council: true or false?

39. Which of the breeds of hobbit was the most common?

40. Minas Morgul was a place of good and healing: true or false?

41. What colour were the faces of the Black Riders?

42. What land feature did Tom Bombadil tell the hobbits to pass on the west-side?

43. Whose 111th birthday party is anticipated in Hobbiton with great excitement?

44. Gandalf and Elrond would not let who return to Hobbiton for fear of the enemy?

45. Which one of the following three hobbits is married: Frodo, Bilbo or Otho?

46. How much did the pony from Bree cost: 6, 12, 18 or 30 silver pennies?

47. Was Aragorn a great huntsman, a great spell-maker, a great musician or a great wizard?

48. Which hobbit had a long and close friendship with the dwarf, Balin?

49. How many of the Black Riders' horses were found after the flood?

50. Where did Ham Gamgee send the Black Rider looking for Mr Baggins: Buckleberry, Woody End or Brandywine Bridge?

QUIZ 4

1. Who did Bilbo Baggins adopt as his heir?

2. What sort of weapon was associated with the name Gil-galad?

3. How many Black Riders in total attempted to attack the hobbits at Weathertop?

4. Who held a Hundredweight Feast in Bilbo's honour?

5. Who comes to rescue the hobbits from Old Man Willow?

6. Cerin Amroth is found in the middle of which wood?

7. Was Fredegar Bolger an enemy, friend or stranger to Frodo?

8. Bonfire Glade can be found in which forest in Middle-earth?

9. On their fifth day out from Bree, the hobbits left behind which set of marshes beginning with the letter M?

10. What is the name of Ham Gamgee's son?

11. In which month did the hobbits and Strider reach Weathertop?

12. Who had once turned trolls into stone?

13. What sort of creature shot and killed Balin?

14. Who smells the blood of living things but cannot see like most creatures?

15. Gwaihir the Windlord was: a bird, a horse, a dwarf messenger or an Elf-king?

16. Were none, some or all of the Company blindfolded as they were taken through Lothlórien?

17. Do the hobbits try to chop down, burn or put a spell on the tree trapping them in the Old Forest?

18. What was the name of the horse Gandalf took from Rohan?

19. The Blue Mountains contained mines that were used by dwarves, goblins or orcs?

20. To whom did Bilbo address the envelope containing the ring?

21. By what name is the Fire-mountain known?

22. Who taught Sam Gamgee to read?

23. Which mines beginning with the letter M, do the Company visit?

24. What is the name of the Lord of the Galadhrim?

25. A store of what object did Sam Gamgee find when searching Weathertop?

26. In which compass direction did the hobbits travel as they set out from Tom Bombadil's house?

27. Over what object do Gandalf and Bilbo argue before Bilbo leaves Bag End?

28. What sort of creature was Ancalagon the Black?

29. The hobbits and Strider cross the Last Bridge; which river does it span?

30. Which member of the Company has to be blindfolded through Lothlórien?

31. What dark creatures did Frodo dream about at Tom Bombadil's house?

32. How were Frodo's father and mother alleged to have died?

33. In whose house did Frodo first try on the ring?

34. From whom did Radagast the Brown bring a message for Gandalf?

35. How many years old is a hobbit when he or she comes of age?

36. What colour hair does Goldberry have?

37. Mithril is the name of a valuable metal, a charmed elven sword or a healing potion?

38. In his letter to Frodo, who does Gandalf suggest may meet Frodo on his journey?

39. What is Fredegar Bolger's nickname?

40. The city of Osgiliath was also known as the Citadel of the Sun, the Stars or the Moon?

41. In which river did Sméagol and his friend recover the ring?

42. Who threw an apple which hit Bill Ferny as the hobbits left Bree?

43. What sort of weapon did Gimli carry with him?

44. What sort of transport did Lord Celeborn provide the Company with?

45. How many ponies arrived at Tom Bombadil's beckoning?

46. What creatures have often stolen the jewels and gold from Moria?

47. Tobold Hornblower of Longbottom was the first to grow what plant?

48. Which friend of Frodo's is to stay behind in the Shire and look after Frodo's affairs?

49. Which pass through the mountains, beginning with the letter R, do the Company attempt to cross?

50. Whose tomb does the Company find in Moria?

1. Who paid for the pony bought by the hobbits in Bree?

2. What did Gandalf do with the ring when Frodo gave it to him?

3. Who is the only member of the Company to have spent time in the Dark Lord's dungeons?

4. Who has a beard, a bright blue coat and yellow boots?

5. Who was the eldest surviving female relative of Bilbo and Frodo?

6. A pair of what kind of trees marked the end of the elven-way from Hollin?

7. Arwen had two brothers, both of whose names started with the letter E. Can you name one?

8. Which wizard visited Frodo at Bag End after a long absence?

9. Who found the hobbits' ponies after they had left Bree and returned them to Mr Butterbur?

10. Who had to decide whether to follow his master or stay with Bill the pony?

11. What event at the dinner did many of Bilbo's birthday party guests dread?

12. How many trolls alarmed Pippin and Merry on their journey from Weathertop?

13. In what language were the letters that appeared on Frodo's ring?

14. What would Frodo have become if the Black Riders had stabbed him through the heart?

15. Sauron the Great is known by what other name?

16. Dwarf doors are invisible when shut: true or false?

17. What is the first meal the hobbits have at Tom Bombadil's house?

18. What type of creature are the three brothers, Haldir, Orophin and Rúmil?

19. What caused Merry to fall to pieces in Bree when he saw the Black Riders: the Curse of Shanor, the Black Breath or the Sword of Erendil?

20. In which month is Frodo Baggins' birthday?

21. Who caught Gollum in the Dead Marshes?

22. What type of flower is Tom Bombadil holding when he meets the hobbits?

23. How many Farthings was the Shire divided into?

24. According to Gandalf, the few remaining Men of the West are: orcs, hobbits, rangers or ringwraiths?

25. Which creatures know Strider by the name Forn?

26. What is the name of the tower in Mordor?

27. Luthien was the daughter of which King of the Elves?

28. Who broke the news that Gollum had escaped from the elves?

29. Which of the hobbits was the first to sing a song in honour of Goldberry?

30. What sort of frightening creature did Gandalf conjure up at Bilbo's birthday party?

31. What material, beginning with the letter M, is Frodo's mail-shirt made of?

32. Ringwraiths are the servants of orcs, the Dark Lord or Tom Bombadil?

33. What item, given to Frodo, was studded with white gems and came with a belt of pearl and crystal?

34. What sort of game did Bilbo and Gollum play as a challenge?

35. Is Lady Galadriel an elf, dwarf, hobbit or female orc?

36. How old was Bilbo when Frodo came to live with him: 69, 99, 109 or 111?

37. Which elf turns out to be the keeper of the ring of Adamant?

38. What sort of creatures helped Gollum escape from the elves by causing a diversion?

39. Nob's hair stood on end when he encountered Gandalf, a Black Rider or Saruman?

40. Do hobbits give or receive presents on their birthday?

41. Radagast the Brown was a member of the same wizard's order as Gandalf: true or false?

42. Old Winyards is a type of pipe tobacco, red wine or ointment?

43. What natural phenomenon do the Black Riders fear?

44. What was the surname of Frodo's friend whose first name was Folco?

45. Gandalf carried a sword and what other item on the journey from Rivendell?

46. What sort of weapon hurt Frodo at Weathertop: a knife, a sword, a wand or a spear?

47. What item of jewellery did Tom Bombadil pick out from the treasure for his partner, Goldberry?

48. According to elven lore, are there seven, nine or eleven rings for the Dwarf-lords?

49. What sort of creature do the Company first encounter in the Golden Wood?

50. Goldberry tells the hobbits that Tom Bombadil is an orc: true or false?

QUIZ 6

1. Do hobbits like heights?

2. Who was imprisoned on the pinnacle of Orthanc?

3. According to elven lore, how many rings are there for the Dark Lord?

4. What is the name of the meeting everyone attends at Rivendell in October?

5. Thorin Oakenshield was a dwarf, human or elf in exile?

6. What piece of jewellery did Lady Galadriel give Aragorn?

7. What position did Will Whitfoot hold in the Shire?

8. How many other people sat down to eat with Frodo, Sam and Pippin at Mr Maggot's house?

9. Was Miss Primula Brandybuck Frodo's wife, mother or grandmother?

10. Does Gandalf describe Frodo as shorter, rounder or taller than some hobbits?

11. Who asks Gandalf to join him in his plan to rule Middle-earth?

12. Who does Frodo climb into the tree with to meet the elves in Golden Wood?

13. What sort of creatures did Frodo think he saw on the tops of the waves at the Ford of Rivendell?

14. What object does Lady Galadriel show Sam and Frodo?

15. What is the name of the seat on the hill of Amon Hen?

16. What name, beginning with the letter D, was given to the doors that led into Moria?

17. What is the name of the Ranger Frodo meets at the Prancing Pony inn?

18. How many hobbits crossed the Brandywine River along with Frodo?

19. Was The Green Dragon a public house for hobbits, a hot dish containing cheese or an ancient runestone?

20. How many years old is a hobbit celebrating its eleventy-first birthday?

21. How many bathtubs had Merry arranged at Crickhollow?

22. Who started to tell strangers at the Prancing Pony inn about Bilbo's birthday party?

23. What happens to Frodo's sword if orcs are close by?

24. Who gave the cordial of Imladris to Gandalf to share out with the others on their journey?

25. Who does Frodo find sitting on a stool with bread and water after the feast at Rivendell?

26. Who owned a sword with a blade broken a foot below the hilt?

27. How many dogs accompanied Farmer Maggot when he encountered Frodo, Sam and Pippin?

28. Who is held in prison by wood-elves?

29. The Mathom-house at Michel Delving is a court, a palace, a museum or a church?

30. What is the surname of the people Frodo sells Bag End to?

31. Which of these was the name of one of Farmer Maggot's dogs: Grab, Gnash, Grip or Grapple?

32. Was Tom Bombadil's pony smaller or larger than the others?

33. Who did Strider meet at Sarn Ford on the first of May, 1418?

34. Which of these people did Frodo not see when he looked into the Mirror of Galadriel: his father, Drogo, Gandalf or Bilbo?

35. Which golden-haired member of the house of Elrond greeted Strider and the hobbits on their journey?

36. How many boats did the Company use to travel on the Silverlode River?

37. Which friend of Frodo Baggins has the full name Meriadoc?

38. What does Gandalf tell Frodo to throw the ring into, to destroy it?

39. What sort of footwear was laid out for the hobbits at Tom Bombadil's house?

40. Who, at the Prancing Pony inn, calls Frodo first Master Underhill and then Mr Baggins?

41. How many gates allow entry through the circle of Isengard?

42. Who led the Company after Gandalf's disappearance into the abyss?

43. Who first discovered that Frodo was wearing a mail shirt?

44. In which town did Bill Ferny live?

45. What was the name of Tom Bombadil's pony?

46. Which gardener overheard Gandalf and Frodo's conversation at Bag End?

47. 'Mellon' is the elvish word for foe, friend, wife or the Dark Lord?

48. Who fled the house at Crickhollow as Black Riders appeared?

49. By what name was Peregrin Took usually called?

50. What was the first name of Frodo's father?

QUIZ 7

1. With what creatures did Bilbo travel on his last trip before settling at Rivendell?

2. What came out of the water to grab Frodo's foot?

3. What sort of creature was Thorin Oakenshield?

4. What was Frodo doing when he disappeared at the Prancing Pony inn?

5. Who came to rescue the hobbits from the barrow?

6. Who met Frodo and the others at the ferry over the Brandywine?

7. Gandalf's meeting with Frodo at Bag End was their first meeting in how many years?

8. Which wizard was famed throughout the Shire for his skill with lights, fires and smoke?

9. What material is the basin of the Mirror of Galadriel made of?

10. For how long had Sam Gamgee tended Bilbo's garden at Bag End?

11. Who fell into the water at Parth Galen trying to stop Frodo leaving on his own?

12. How many people did Frodo live with in Bag End after Bilbo's departure: none, one or three?

13. There are still dragons in Middle-earth according to Gandalf: true or false?

14. With what weapon did Frodo attack the hand that crawled towards his friends in the barrow?

15. What does Strider ask for in return for telling Frodo important information?

16. Who was king of the Dwarf-kingdom: Dáin, Glóin or Nori?

17. How many steps did the Company count as they climbed up from the Doors of Durin into Moria?

18. Who gave Frodo his sword for the journey from Rivendell?

19. Which hobbit family lived at Number 3 Bagshot Row?

20. Nen Hithoel is: a small river, a pale lake, a forested hill or a stone cave?

21. Who started out in a boat with Merry and Pippin?

22. The Withywindle joins which other river below Haysend?

23. Does the orc chieftan strike Frodo's left or right side whilst battling in Moria?

24. Pippin and Merry were not part of the Company of the Ring: true or false?

25. How many feet in height do hobbits seldom exceed?

26. What old, worn out item of clothing too big for Bilbo did he put on after his birthday party?

27. Did Bilbo come across the ring in a lake, a mine or a forest?

28. What name, beginning with the letter D, did Bilbo call Strider?

29. Who was the last person to see Bilbo before he left Bag End on his travels?

30. What creature emerges from among the orcs as the Company is about to cross the bridge in Moria?

31. Barliman Butterbur is the keeper of which inn?

32. Who cured Frodo of the wound inflicted at Weathertop?

33. Who does Frodo suspect has been following them since Moria?

34. Where was Frodo when he used the ring for the second time?

35. Who, along with Aragorn, clears a path through the snowdrift for the others to pass?

36. Which of the hobbits first spotted Black Riders in the village of Bree?

37. In which month did the scouts sent to discover news of the Black Riders and other evil powers start to return?

38. Who created the flood at the Ford of Rivendell?

39. In what year did Frodo set out on his adventure?

40. What was placed around the waists of Pippin, Sam and Merry in the barrow?

41. What is the name of the tree that tries to trap the hobbits?

42. Who was the figure bathed in white light at the Ford of Rivendell?

43. Who does Gandalf say has become master of Bag End in Bilbo's absence?

44. Which river does the Silverlode River flow into?

45. What item did Bilbo leave Adelard Took as a present?

46. What was the name given to anything that a hobbit had no use for but didn't throw away?

47. The Sickle is the hobbits' name for which constellation of stars?

48. Which member of Frodo's party disappeared from the banks of the Withywindle?

49. Which of the following symbols were not found on the Doors of Durin: an anvil, an axe, a hammer or a star?

50. Who represented the elves in the Company of the Ring?

QUIZ 8

1. Where do Bob and Nob work?

2. What word in English acted as the password to open the doors into Moria?

3. The Tower of the Setting Sun was also known by what name?

4. Which hill does Strider suggest Frodo and the others should head for?

5. What did Frodo claim had thrown him into the River Withywindle?

6. Are hobbits bigger or smaller than dwarves?

7. The peak of Tol Brandir lies just beyond which set of pillars?

8. Is Esgalduin: a famous minstrel, a troll king, a magic shield or an enchanted river?

9. What happened to Bilbo at the end of his birthday party dinner?

10. What is the name of the city where the Galadhrim elves live?

11. Who does Tom Bombadil say is waiting for him?

12. In what sort of dwelling did all hobbits originally live?

13. What does Gandalf set alight to ward off the Wargs?

14. Which of the breeds of hobbit were the shortest: Stoors, Harfoots or Fallohides?

15. Which Ranger is the son of Arathorn?

16. What is the first settlement that the hobbits encounter after parting with Tom Bombadil?

17. Bamfurlong is land owned by which farmer?

18. How many signatures from witnesses have to feature on a hobbit legal document?

19. Do most hobbits reach 100, 150 or 200 years of age?

20. What weapon did the figures on the Pillars of the Kings hold?

21. Hobbits' feet are leathery and covered with hair: true or false?

22. Which hobbit was trapped around the waist by a tree?

23. Who does the verse in Gandalf's letter to Frodo refer to?

24. Which member of Frodo's party had never crossed the Brandywine River before?

25. Who did Elendil of Westernesse help to overthrow?

26. The Stoors were the hobbits most friendly to dwarves: true or false?

27. Who asked Mr Butterbur to keep a look out for Frodo?

28. How many people were invited to Bilbo's birthday dinner party: 48, 64 or 144?

29. Who was the first to greet Frodo at his new home in Crickhollow?

30. What enveloped the hobbits in the Old Forest causing Frodo to lose contact with the others?

31. Sauron's ring was cut from his hand by the son of Gil-galad, Isildur Elendil or Drogo Baggins?

32. Were the men of Westernee partners with or opponents of the Dark Lord?

33. Which of these people did not ask for a private talk with Frodo at the Prancing Pony inn: Mr Mugwort, Mr Butterbur or Strider?

34. Andúril, Flame of the West was the name that Aragorn gave to what object?

35. Which member of the Company attacks Frodo to try and gain the ring?

36. How many, apart from Frodo, set out from Rivendell with the ring?

37. Arwen was the daughter of the Lord of Rivendell: what was his name?

38. By what name does Frodo Baggins want to be known to strangers?

39. What was the name the hobbits called their police?

40. Did orcs, trolls or the ringwraiths kill Isildur Elendil with arrows?

41. Where did Frodo find himself after encountering a Barrow-wight?

42. Whose knees did the Balrog's whip wrap around, drawing him into the abyss?

43. What was the name of the creature Sméagol killed to get hold of the ring?

44. Which one of the Company is unhappy to enter the Golden Wood?

45. What colour clothing were Frodo's friends wearing when he found them in the barrow?

46. Who ran the fireworks for Bilbo's birthday party?

47. Into which forest do the hobbits head after leaving Crickhollow?

48. Wargs are servants of the Dark Lord: true or false?

49. The region that men call Hollin is known as what by elves?

50. At which inn do the hobbits and Strider all sleep in the same room for safety?

QUIZ 9

1. Caras Galadhon is: an ally of Sauron, a river in Hobbiton or a hill?

2. Who sold Frodo and the hobbits a pony in Bree?

3. In which mountain range would you find Caradhras, Silvertine and Cloudyhead?

4. Which breed of hobbit is beardless and prefers highlands and hillsides: Harfoots, Stoors or Fallohides?

5. Did white wolves, grey bears or black orcs cross the frozen Brandywine River in the Fell Winter of 1311?

6. How many elf-towers could still be seen on the Tower Hills from the Shire?

7. The Mirror of Galadriel was found in Moria, Lothlórien or the Old Forest?

8. What item in Frodo's possession is referred to as Isildur's Bane?

9. Did the hobbits finally leave Bree at 10 o'clock, 2 o'clock or 4 o'clock?

10. Which member of the Company confronted a Balrog on a bridge at Moria?

11. Which hobbit, apart from Frodo, has read some of Bilbo Baggins' book?

12. Who was 100 years old when she finally claimed ownership of Bag End?

13. What colour were the clothes laid out for Frodo when he awoke at Rivendell?

14. Is the village of Tuckborough found in Eregion, Rohan or Hobbiton?

15. How many Black Riders were on the Bridge of Mitheithel when Glorfindel first rode there?

16. What handy climbing item did Sam remind himself several times to pack for the journey?

17. Farmer Maggot had a large dog called Fang: true or false?

18. Frodo fell asleep as which hobbit recited a long poem at Rivendell?

19. What item of jewellery did Bilbo use to leave his own birthday party?

20. Was Legolas an elf, dwarf, hobbit or orc?

21. How many nights did Frodo spend at his new home at Crickhollow before starting his quest?

22. Elrond's mother was: Elendil, Isaldor, Goldberry or Elwing?

23. What is the name, beginning with the letter R, of the lands of the Horse-lords?

24. Mr Butterbur would leave Bree given any chance: true or false?

25. Which years of age are a hobbit's 'tweens': 8-15, 12-20 or 20-33?

26. Were the lower levels of Moria: ablaze with fire, buried under an avalanche or flooded, during the Company's time there?

27. Who urges Frodo to head to Minas Tirith with him?

28. What blind creature did Gollum catch and eat raw?

29. What sort of land feature is the Celebrant?

30. With which dwarf did Legolas the elf initially quarrel on the Company's travels?

31. Bagshot Row contained two, three, five or twelve dwellings?

32. Whose heart was nearly pierced by a Morgul-knife?

33. Which hobbit dropped a stone down a well in Moria and was told off by Gandalf?

34. Who did the hobbits meet in the Old Forest wearing a green gown and a belt of gold?

35. In 1342, Bilbo left the Shire, returned to the Shire or was born in the Shire?

36. To what water feature, beginning with the letter R, does Aragorn suggest the Company take their boats?

37. Where did Frodo discover the ring on his body after awaking at Rivendell?

38. Daddy Twofoot is The Gamgees', the Baggins' or the Brandybucks' next-door neighbour?

39. The Hedge is a boundary which marks the end of what area of land dear to hobbits?

40. Who owned the last house in the village of Bree and housed a mysterious southerner?

41. What sort of creature has Sam Gamgee longed to see for many years?

42. What was the surname of the brothers Marcho and Blanco: Saruman, Baggins, Fallohide or Brandybuck?

43. By what other name is the mountain of Barazinbar known?

44. What relation is Bilbo to Angelica Baggins?

45. At which inn were models of the hobbits placed in what were supposed to be their beds?

46. Is Celebdil the White a mountain, an Elf-king or a wizard?

47. The trees in the Old Forest move their branches at will: true or false?

48. Which hobbit looked into the Mirror of Galadriel first?

49. Baranduin is another name for which river?

50. The Fallohides preferred woodlands, mountains or lowlands?

Questions about The Two Towers

1. Who threw a ball from Orthanc, which just missed Gandalf?

2. With what object did Sam hit Gollum's arm fiercely?

3. Is the Lady of Rohan called Éowyn, Éudor or Elrond?

4. Which two members of the Company of the Ring were friendly rivals over how many enemies they had slain?

5. What is the name of the city of the Men of Númenor?

6. What is a gathering of ents called?

7. What creatures slain by Boromir had slant eyes, bows made of yew and short swords?

8. Bregalad means: Quicksilver, Quicktongue, Quickbeam or Quickfoot in hobbit language?

9. A lunge at Shelob's stomach was Sam's first, second, third or fourth attack with the sword?

10. The orcs bound Pippin by cords around the legs, wrists and where else?

11. Éomer's sword was called Andúril, Sting or Gúthwine?

12. The gardens made by the entwives but now barren are known by what name?

13. Théoden left the Hornburg to attack the Isengard forces at dawn, midday, sunset or midnight?

14. Every month in the Shire calendar has the same number of days; how many are there?

15. What sort of creature does Gorbag think is still loose near to Minas Morgul?

16. What is the name of the food, beginning with the letter L, which Gimli, Legolas and Aragorn ate as they pursued the hobbits?

17. Lebethron is: a sacred drink, a tree, a type of nourishing bread or a temple?

18. Which hobbit witnesses Gollum debating out loud whether he should steal the ring?

19. Which wizard arrived with Erkenbrand and a thousand men at Helm's Dike?

20. Which is longest – the Straight Stair or the Winding Stair?

21. Which hobbit made the sound of Gollum to convince an orc he had the ring?

22. The Hourns are related to: ents, orcs, men of Rohan or dwarves?

23. What is the name of the sly adviser to Théoden?

24. Sam referred to the two minds of which creatures as 'stinker' and 'slinker'?

25. What is the name of the horn that sounds at the start of the book?

26. What colour are Saruman's beard and hair?

27. Which evil power claimed lordship over the lands of the riders of Rohan?

28. In which compass direction did the Window of the Sunset face?

29. Are ents stronger or weaker than trolls?

30. Shelob only drinks cold blood, eats the meat of living creatures or eats dead creatures?

31. Which creature tries but cannot eat the elf's bread that Sam and Frodo have?

32. Who did Aragorn find hurt near the lake and about a mile from Parth Galen?

33. Who lets slip to Faramir that Boromir tried to take the ring from Frodo?

34. What did Gandalf house the glass ball in: a wooden box, a shroud made of chain mail, a cloth or a knapsack?

35. Gimli, Legolas and Aragorn abandon the boats and the river to set off after what creature by foot?

36. Did the main battle between the orcs and Riders of Rohan occur at: midday, midnight, sunrise or sunset?

37. Which two members of the Company sat high up on top of an arch watching Isengard being flooded?

38. What type of creature had Shelob had to feast on for many years?

39. After climbing the two sets of stairs, do the hobbits and Gollum then pass through a tunnel, over a bridge or down a stream?

40. Whose symbol is a white hand on a black background and the letter S?

41. Who tried but failed to cut through the cobwebs in Shelob's Lair?

42. What did Saruman tell the men of Dunland happened to prisoners of the Rohan?

43. Lord Celeborn warned the Company about which forest?

44. The palantíri were used as communications devices to keep the kingdom of Gondor together: true or false?

45. What is the name of the pillar shaped like a body part, which once stood at Isengard?

46. What is unusual about the way that Legolas sleeps?

47. What symbol did Frodo, Sam and Gollum find on occasion carved into fallen trees?

48. What sort of weapon had pierced Boromir many times?

49. Torech Ungol is also known as whose lair?

50. Is Gandalf allowed to keep his staff before going to meet Théoden?

QUIZ 2

1. What is the name of the glass ball that is thrown at Gandalf at Isengard?

2. Which hobbit launched into the history of pipeweed and pipe smoking in front of Théoden and others at Isengard?

3. What happened to the staff when Sam hit Gollum's back with it?

4. Which weapon did the Riders of Rohan not carry: tall spears, heavy axes, long swords or painted shields?

5. What magical thing did the rope do after Sam and Frodo had climbed down Emyn Muil?

6. Which hobbit had a cut on his forehead which left him with a permanent scar?

7. How many of Frodo's party does Faramir insist must be blindfolded when led away from Henneth Annûn?

8. The Winged Messengers are the new incarnation of what evil creature?

9. Who did Saruman try to convince, from his tower, to join forces with him: Treebeard, Frodo, Théoden or Legolas?

10. Gandalf is not popular in Rohan because he took: a sacred sword, a sacred book, a sacred horse or a sacred crystal?

11. From what land were the two men soldiers called Mablung and Damrod?

12. What is the name of the entwife that Treebeard would most like to see again?

13. Who offers Gandalf, Gimli, Legolas and Aragorn armour before they head to Isengard?

14. According to the orcs, who are Sauron's favourites?

15. Old Gerontius was Pippin, Merry, Sam or Frodo's great-great-grandfather?

16. Hama, Théoden's captain, died, was injured or fled the battle at Helm's Gate?

17. Gandalf, Aragorn and the others are asked to leave their weapons before meeting Théoden: true or false?

18. Isengarders and Northerners were groups of elves, orcs, black riders or dwarves?

19. Frodo and Sam saw a battle between men from Harad and men from which other land?

20. Nan Curunir is known as the Valley of what?

21. Approximately how many ents did Pippin and Merry spot at the gathering in Fangorn: 12, 24, 36 or 48?

22. Cirion was the 11th, 12th, 13th or 14th Steward of the Men of Númenor?

23. The fifth of March was the date when: Frodo disappeared, Gandalf and the others found Merry and Pippin, or Hama died?

24. Faramir urges Frodo and Sam not to drink water that comes from which valley?

25. What was the name of the set of caves which had impressed Gimli greatly in Rohan?

26. Who recites a Shire poem about Oliphaunts?

27. Who asks Gimli to ride on his horse to Isengard?

28. What does Treebeard name the new forest that will surround Orthanc?

29. What was the name, beginning with the letter H, of the horse lent to Aragorn by the riders of Rohan?

30. What unit of measurement, beginning with the letter E, do the hobbits use to measure rope?

31. Which creatures first woke trees up and taught them to talk?

32. Éomer knelt before Théoden and offered what object of his to the ruler?

33. What is Ephel Dúath: an ancient ent curse, a mountain range, Sauron's deadly sword or a small elf township?

34. What name did Sam give to the creature the soldiers of Gondor call a Mûmak?

35. Who suddenly lifted Merry and Pippin up when they were wandering alone through Fangorn?

36. What item does Frodo manage to grab instead of the ring as he watches the army leave Minas Morgul?

37. Who is the master of Westfold and lives in the Hornburg at Helm's Gate?

38. What evidence of Merry and Pippin being alive does Aragorn spot alongside a mallorn-leaf?

39. What is the name of the orc, beginning with the letter G, who suspects that Pippin and Merry have the ring with them?

40. How long is the rope in Sam Gamgee's pack: 10 ells, 30 ells, 50 ells or 90 ells?

41. How many figures did Théoden and the others spot at the ruined gate of Isengard?

42. What decoration was on the Mûmak's tusks?

43. What is the name that ents give to their children?

44. Which one of these three sites did not possess a palantíri stone: Minas Tirith, Minas Ithil or Minas Anor?

45. When Gandalf whistled, what creatures came to the Fangorn?

46. Which ent chased Saruman back into the tower of Orthanc?

47. The hobbits didn't eat the meat from the orcs as they couldn't tell from what creature it came: true or false?

48. What colour is the tower guarding the pass into Mordor that the hobbits and Gollum are travelling along?

49. Who does Gandalf insist Théoden summons before he will explain his plans?

50. Orcs cannot normally endure bright sunlight: true or false?

QUIZ 3

1. Which, out of Ithilien, Eriador or the Iron Hills, were lands largely controlled by the Men of Númenor?

2. Who led a group into Orthanc to meet Saruman?

3. Which of the Company entered Shelob's Lair first?

4. Which member of the Company of the Ring received a head wound whilst fighting at Helm's Gate?

5. Who calls the sun 'Yellow Face': Treebeard, Sauron, Gollum or Tom Bombadil?

6. Who does Faramir call the Grey Pilgrim?

7. How many toes does Treebeard have on each of his feet?

8. What is the name, beginning with the letter H, of the Doorward of Théoden?

9. Faramir's father is the 13th, 20th, 26th or 36th Steward?

10. Did Gollum insist that he, Sam and Frodo travel by day or by night?

11. Who do the orcs call Shelob's Sneak?

12. How many people were in the group that went to Orthanc to meet with Saruman?

13. By what two words, both starting with the letter G, do the riders of Rohan call Gandalf?

14. Where did the winged creature head after passing right over Sam, Frodo and Gollum in the marshes?

15. To the elves, Gandalf is known by what name, beginning with the letter M?

16. Who cried 'Elendil' and confronted the riders of Rohan?

17. Was Sam, Frodo or Gollum the most exhausted as they travelled across the marshes?

18. What tower was built on four black piers and stood in the centre of Isengard?

19. What sort of tool did Pippin use to cut the cords that bound his wrists?

20. The noldor, men of Rohan, ents or orcs made the palantíri in ancient times?

21. Théoden offered the members of the Company of the Ring armour: who took none?

22. Which member of the Company finds a pile of five dead orcs, with two beheaded?

23. Where on their journey with Gollum do Sam and Frodo see faces and strange lights?

24. What type of creature attacked and killed Boromir?

25. Shelob has more than one type of poison: true or false?

26. Which is the only horse Gandalf would ride without a saddle and bridle?

27. Who was head of the original White Council: Sauron, Saruman, Galadriel or Gandalf?

28. Barad-dûr is found in which land in Middle-earth?

29. Which character is searching for Frodo at the very start of **The Two Towers**?

30. Who had placed dried fruits, salted meats and bread in Sam and Frodo's packs for their journey?

31. Sauron allows his followers to speak and write his true name: true or false?

32. What is the name of the weapon with which Frodo forced Gollum to let go of Sam?

33. Meduseld is the Golden Hall of which ruler?

34. Sauron sent prisoners to Shelob to be eaten: true or false?

35. How many people capable of fighting were already at Helm's Gate before Théoden's forces arrived?

36. How many goblin-soldiers did Aragorn and the others find amongst the dead orcs at Parth Galen?

37. Pippin gave which member of the Company his spare wooden pipe?

38. What did Frodo hold in his left hand as he advanced towards the many eyes in Shelob's Lair?

39. Which member of the Company rode a horse without a saddle?

40. How many roads does Frodo spot winding to the Gate of Mordor?

41. Which member of the Company of the Ring had visited Isengard and seen Pippin and Merry there?

42. According to Treebeard, the Great Wars mainly concern men and which other creature?

43. Both Frodo and Sam are given what wooden item from Faramir?

44. Gimli, Legolas and Aragorn decided to follow Frodo by boat: true or false?

45. What creatures are giant shepherds of trees?

46. What does Gollum call the lights that Sam and Frodo see in the marshes?

47. Did Aragorn and Éomer first attack a catapult, a siege tower or a battering ram?

48. Whose motto is 'Do not be hasty'?

49. By what mode of transport did Wormtongue reach Isengard?

50. Which member of the Company killed more than 20 orcs before being killed himself?

QUIZ 4

1. Was Frodo dead, bound in cords, asleep or missing a hand when Sam reached Frodo and Shelob?

2. Who does Théoden declare his heir before the journey to Isengard?

3. The Dome of Stars was once found at Rivendell, Osgiliath or Isengard?

4. Was Éomer's father Isildgur, Gandalf, Éomund or Treebeard?

5. Did Sauron, men of Gondor, the riders of Rohan or Saruman originally build the Teeth of Mordor?

6. Orcs like to march under the sun: true or false?

7. According to Pippin, what was the name of the ent, beginning with the letter B, who was burned by Saruman's weapons?

8. What new feature of the land at Helm's Dike suddenly appeared and trapped the orcs?

9. What does Faramir correctly guess caused a problem between Frodo and Boromir?

10. Who held Sting in his right hand as he walked through Shelob's Lair?

11. Uglúk was a Northerner orc, an Isengarder orc or an Eastern Desert orc?

12. What part was the giant statue at the crossroads missing?

13. What sort of food from the elves is flat and wrapped in leaves?

14. There were no guards at Cirith Gorgor: true or false?

15. How many different roads met at the crossroads near Minas Morgul?

16. Which member of the Company deduced that Frodo took one of their boats?

17. Which one of these places is not in Mordor: Erid Lithui, Gorgoroth or Erebor?

18. Isildur, the son of Elendir built which tower?

19. After the battle at Helm's Gate, how many of the enemy had Legolas slain?

20. What was the barrier at the end of the tunnel of Shelob's Lair?

21. What hobbits' weapons did Legolas, Aragorn and Gimli find when searching the dead orcs?

22. What relation is Lady Rohan to Éomer?

23. Which one of the following is not a name for Gandalf: Incánus, Tharkûn, Eldeón or Olórin?

24. Orcs were made by the evil powers in mockery of which creatures?

25. Sam overheard the orcs saying that Frodo was alive, dead or had escaped?

26. Who joined Aragorn kneeling beside the dead body of Boromir?

27. Who held the phial of Galadriel when Shelob appeared in the open?

28. What compass direction were Frodo, Sam and Gollum going to take at the crossroads?

29. Sam's pack still contained two cooking pans by the time they had travelled into Mordor: true or false?

30. Did Sam Gamgee obtain rope to put in his pack from the boats, from the Council at Rivendell or from the ents in Fangorn?

31. The last time the ents were under threat was when the Men of the Sea fought who?

32. Which of these items was not in Sam's pack: a two-pronged knife, pepper, a wooden spoon or salt?

33. How many Winged Messengers are there in total?

34. What creatures used dams to break down Saruman's fortress?

35. What name, beginning with the letter L, do the orcs use to refer to the Dark Tower?

36. What was the name of the rapids where the Company released the body of Boromir?

37. What place with a tower is found in the mountains of Ephel Dúath?

38. How many ents followed Treebeard when Merry and Pippin spotted them?

39. What food apart from dried strips of meat did the orcs give to their hobbit prisoners?

40. Who grabbed Sam just as he was about to warn Frodo of Shelob's arrival?

41. What is the name, beginning with the letter B, of the ent who accompanies the hobbits whilst the Entmoot is on?

42. Sam, Gollum and Frodo spent a night resting in a giant oak tree: true or false?

43. Which member of the Company was unhappy on horses and sat with Legolas?

44. How many exits are there from the rocky chamber that is Faramir and his men's refuge?

45. What creatures are entrusted with keeping Saruman trapped in Orthanc?

46. How many left Théoden's court to travel to Isengard: 100, 1000, 10,000 or 100,000?

47. Ninnyhammer was a nickname that whose father had given to him for being forgetful?

48. Where do Gimli, Legolas and Aragorn start to track the orcs from: Rivendell, Parth Galen or Fangorn?

49. What was the main ingredient of Sam's meal for Frodo that he called stewed coney?

50. Who meets Gimli, Legolas and Aragorn dressed in white with a wide-brimmed hat?

QUIZ 5

1. How many riders does Legolas spy heading across Rohan to meet the Company: 25, 55, 105 or 505?

2. The Great Battle where Sauron was overthrown was fought upon Dagorlad, Erendor or the plains of Mordor?

3. A white running horse on a green background is the symbol of which house?

4. According to Treebeard, the ents and entwives will only meet again when both groups have lost all they had: true or false?

5. Orcs do not drink water: true or false?

6. The inland sea of Núrnen is found in which region of Middle-earth?

7. Who is charged with leading those who don't fight at Isengard to safety?

8. What was the name of the captain of the men of Gondor who met with Frodo and Sam?

9. Alongside which river do Pippin and Merry walk after escaping from the orcs?

10. According to the poet in Rohan, Felaróf was the father of horses, father of kings or father of the lands?

11. Éomer calls men of his own household: éored, éomers, émer or émors?

12. What relation was Faramir to Boromir?

13. The Hornburg has fallen twice to attacks: true or false?

14. What item of jewellery belonging to a hobbit did Aragorn find in the grass of Rohan?

15. Who obtained a Silmaril from the Iron Crown in Thangorodrim?

16. Who do Sam and Frodo spot climbing down Emyn Muil shortly after them?

17. Whose axe became notched when he attacked an orc wearing an iron collar?

18. Who used the phial of Galadriel to finally repel Shelob?

19. What did Treebeard do at night when the hobbits slept?

20. Who cast a spell at Orthanc so that his words sounded sweet and reasonable?

21. Which member of the Company of the Ring does Faramir call High Warden of the White Tower?

22. What creatures approached Sam as he was close to the Cleft?

23. What weapons did both Uglúk and the man who killed him use to battle?

24. Did the men of Dunland fight on the side of Théoden or of Saruman at Helm's Gate?

25. What word, beginning with the letter P, means 'that which looks far away'?

26. Which hobbit lures Gollum away from the forbidden pool at Henneth Annûn?

27. Angrenost is another name for which wizard's home?

28. After leaving Isengard, where do Théoden, Aragorn and the others intend to head?

29. Who sent Gwaihir the Windlord to search for Gandalf?

30. Which wizard is the only one who really cares about trees, according to Treebeard?

31. For how long does Faramir grant Frodo free passage throughout Gondor?

32. Who calls Sam, 'Samwise the stouthearted'?

33. How many times had Gollum visited Mordor before he met Sam and Frodo?

34. How many of the first ents apart from Treebeard are still around?

35. What sort of creatures are Shagrat and Gorbag?

36. What sort of creature was Grishnákh: a rider of Rohan, an orc, an ent or a dwarf?

37. By what device did Sauron communicate with Saruman?

38. Which three of these herbs does Sam ask Gollum to look for: bay leaves, oregano, basil, thyme, mint, sage or rosemary?

39. By what name, beginning with the letter H, did the orcs refer to the hobbits?

40. Gollum is safe in Gondor only as long as he is seen with which hobbit?

41. Four orcs carried whose body on their shoulders to the Undergate?

42. In which mountain range would you find Methedras?

43. Who does Gandalf give the glass ball to in order to keep it safe?

44. Where did Gimli, Aragorn and the others reunite with Merry and Pippin?

45. Cirith Ungol is a high pass through the Ash Mountains, the Mountains of Shadow or the Misty Mountains?

46. On hearing of Aragorn's long and fast journey, what name does Éomer give Aragorn?

47. Who mentioned the star-glass repeatedly whilst in Shelob's Lair?

48. Where does Frodo tell Gollum they are heading?

49. The orcs wounded which ent in the past: Fladrif, Fangorn or Finglas?

50. Which member of the Company fell from Durin Bridge in Moria?

QUIZ 6

1. What item is described as a 'light when all other lights go out'?

2. How many thousand ent-strides did Treebeard travel to take the hobbits to his house?

3. Éomer threatened death to which member of Theoden's court?

4. Pippin and Gandalf travel on Shadowfax to which city?

5. Who managed to cut through the giant cobwebs in Shelob's Lair?

6. Are there three, five or seven riderless horses amongst the group of Rohan riders that reaches Legolas, Gimli and Aragorn?

7. In what set of barren hills do Sam and Frodo get lost for a number of days?

8. Is Firefoot Éomer's sword, his wife, his horse or his servant?

9. Henneth Annûn is a waterfall, a cave, a temple or a sheer cliff?

10. How many seats do you traditionally find in an ent-house?

11. What strikes Frodo and Sam most about the entrance to Shelob's Lair?

12. Around which part of Gollum did Sam tie the rope?

13. Which soldier of Gondor was the first to spot the boat carrying the body of Boromir?

14. Who caught Wormtongue at Isengard?

15. What was the name of the leader of a group of orcs not encircled by the riders of Rohan but nearby?

16. Wormtongue is given two choices by Théoden. One is to flee, what is the other?

17. Finglas, also known as Leaflock, is what kind of creature?

18. Sam's second blow with a sword hit what part of Shelob?

19. What did Pippin wrap up and place beside Gandalf whilst he was sleeping?

20. What did the riders of Rohan do with the bodies of the orcs they killed?

21. Gandalf leaves the army before they reach Isengard: true or false?

22. Whose house is near the base of the Last Mountain?

23. Treebeard met with which member of the Company of the Ring shortly before Saruman's fortress was broken through?

24. What does Faramir insist he must do to Sam and Frodo before he can take them further on their journey?

25. Into which dim and airless forest did Merry and Pippin travel?

26. What ancient trench and rampart is just two furlongs away from Helm's Gate?

27. What was in front of the gate made of rock to which Faramir led Sam and Frodo?

28. Where does Sauron think the Orthanc-stone and Pippin are both housed?

29. The Orcs did not fight the hobbits when they ran into them in the woods, even when Merry cut off several of their arms: true or false?

30. What is Gollum hunting for at the forbidden pool at Henneth Annûn?

31. What is the name of the Orc, beginning with the letter L, who is ordered to guard the hobbits?

32. What was the name of the horse Théoden rode to Isengard: Shadowbane, Snowbane or Silverbane?

33. Which two of the following went to Orthanc to meet with Saruman: Frodo, Théoden, Treebeard, Merry or Aragorn?

34. Which two hobbits were held captive by orcs?

35. Who does Faramir call the Mistress of Magic?

36. What was the title of Théoden's son Théodred?

37. Were there 17, 27, 37 or 47 stone steps leading to the doorway of Orthanc?

38. Did the horses lent to Gimli, Aragorn and Legolas disappear at night or in the day?

39. The High Nazgûl led a large army away from Minas Morgul: true or false?

40. Which man of Númenor urges Frodo not to travel to Cirith Ungol?

41. Herugrim is the ancient sword that belongs to which leader?

42. Frodo, Sam and Gollum heard a loud screech and giant armies head from which tower?

43. Who has Théoden's sword under lock and key?

44. Who was the first person to wear the ring after Frodo?

45. Where did an arrow from a rider of Rohan first hit and hurt Grishnákh?

46. What two items does Gandalf ask Saruman to surrender to him?

47. What colour is the eye painted on the Northern orcs' shields?

48. Which creature do Faramir and Frodo spot in the waters of Henneth Annûn?

49. Who communicated with Pippin via the glass ball?

50. How tall was Treebeard: at least seven feet, at least nine feet, at least eleven feet or at least fourteen feet high?

QUIZ 7

1. Shelob had lived long before Sauron: true or false?

2. Which two of these items were worn by the men of Gondor: green knapsacks, green masks, green gauntlets or green armour?

3. Which of these names are not ones given to Treebeard: Fangorn, Ent or Denuidin?

4. At the start of their journey with Gollum, how many weeks does Sam tell Frodo he thinks their elf-bread will last?

5. Who had killed the mount of a Winged Messenger with an arrow?

6. How many palantíri stones apart from the Orthanc-stone were made?

7. Who does Gandalf say is the oldest living, walking creature in Middle-earth?

8. In four days, Gimli, Legolas and Aragorn travelled: 24 leagues, 30 leagues, 45 leagues or 60 leagues?

9. The Deeping Wall was ten feet, twenty feet, thirty feet or fifty feet high?

10. How many entrances were there to Orthanc tower?

11. What item of Boromir's does Frodo mention to Faramir to prove he knew him?

12. What item did Sam use to let Frodo climb up the cliff to safety?

13. What had Merry and Pippin been doing just before they met with Gandalf and the others?

14. What was the name of the eagle sent ahead by Gandalf to search for news?

15. What is the name of Treebeard's language?

16. Who, according to Uglúk, gives the Orcs man's-flesh for food?

17. Whose body did Gandalf, Merry and the others discover rigid and on its back the night after they left Isengard?

18. What item did the orcs wield to punish the hobbits: a branding iron, handcuffs, a whip or a heavy weight?

19. Gollum first leads Sam and Frodo into: a mountain range, marshes, a forest or across a lake?

20. Who rode with Gandalf on the horse, Shadowfax, to the halls of Théoden?

21. What nickname, beginning with the letter W, do the orcs give the riders of Rohan?

22. Which member of the Company was Treebeard reluctant to invite to the forest?

23. The Lady of Lorien had given the Company: jugs of mead, a honey potion, a strength-reviving bread or a slab of cured meat?

24. Gandalf accused Wormtongue of being under whose command?

25. Where did Pippin discover two barrels of the finest pipeweed called Longbottom Leaf?

26. According to Gandalf, where does the enemy think that the Company are all heading?

27. What relation is Théoden to Éomer?

28. What did Frodo tie the rope to before lowering Sam down the cliff at Emyn Muil?

29. After finding rabbits, what is the next errand Sam asks Gollum to do?

30. Shadowfax never returned to Rohan after being ridden away by Gandalf: true or false?

31. Who took the ring from Frodo's unconscious body and placed it around his own neck?

32. Which three members of the Company are fed by Merry and Pippin at Isengard?

33. How many people accompany Théoden when Gandalf and the others meet him?

34. Which former enemies of the Men of Númenor help them by guarding their northern marches?

35. Shelob managed to sting which one of the hobbits?

36. The pipeweed that Merry and Pippin discovered came from which part of Middle-earth?

37. What is the punishment for entering Henneth Annûn without an invitation?

38. Who do the orcs at Minas Morgul describe as elvish but undersized?

39. The riders of Rohan lent Gimli, Legolas and Aragorn how many horses?

40. Where did Sam and Frodo catch sight of many terrifying eyes all looking at them?

41. What is the name, beginning with the letter N, given to the winged messengers of Mordor?

42. What rude action did Wormtongue do at Théoden's feet before he fled?

43. The riders of Rohan are familiar with and have met hobbits in the past: true or false?

44. Gandalf unveils Grima, son of Gálmód, as the real name of whom?

45. The two towers which guard the entrance to Cirith Gorgor are known by what name?

46. What weapon was used to finally kill Grishnákh?

47. Beleriand was the place where which sword was forged?

48. Osgiliath lay east, west or south of the crossroads that Gollum led Sam and Frodo to?

49. As Sam, Frodo and Gollum enter Mordor, which mountains are to the West?

50. What is the name of the commander of the orcs who holds Pippin and Merry prisoner?

QUIZ 8

1. Imlad Morgul is known by what other chilling name?

2. Who killed the orcs that had taken Merry and Pippin?

3. Shelob only ate dwarves and hobbits: true or false?

4. Which hobbit's footprints does Aragorn first detect in the grass of Rohan?

5. In what compass direction did Frodo, Sam and Gollum head from the Gate of Mordor?

6. Cirith Gorgor is known by what ghostly other name?

7. Who had Gollum gone to meet before the hobbits entered Shelob's Lair?

8. What did Gollum do when Sam tied the rope around him?

9. Which orc poured a hot burning liquid down Pippin's throat to revive him?

10. When Gandalf cast Saruman from the order and the Council, he also broke what item?

11. Which rider of Rohan was titled the Third Marshal of Riddermark?

12. Which member of the Company believed that the old man spotted in Fangorn is Saruman?

13. Who was the first to arrive at Isengard after the waters had damaged the fortress?

14. Which stair do the hobbits and Gollum climb first: the Straight Stair or the Winding Stair?

15. The usual orc sword is a curved scimitar, a long-bladed rapier or a short-bladed sword?

16. By what name does Faramir refer to the ring that is in Frodo's possession?

17. How many rode from Helm's Gate to Isengard with Gandalf: fewer than ten, fewer than thirty, fewer than fifty or more than fifty?

18. Which rider of Rohan killed Uglúk?

19. Who did Pippin ride with after they had seen the Nazgûl in the night sky?

20. Where did the Entmoot decide to travel to?

21. What was the name of the group of orcs in charge of the mission to capture the hobbits?

22. What protective item other than an iron and leather hat did Gimli take from Théoden's collection?

23. On what river, beginning with the letter A, did Faramir see his dead brother's body?

24. Which river was diverted to attack Saruman's fortress: the Brandywine, the Isen, the Entwash or the Anduin?

25. The old man who appeared in front of Gimli, Legolas and Aragorn lent on what item?

26. Who took charge of Isengard straight after Saruman was overthrown?

27. In what did Aragorn, Gimli and Legolas place the body of Boromir?

28. What food did Gollum bring back from the woods for Sam and Frodo?

29. Who sliced off one of Shelob's claws with a blow from the sword, Sting?

30. Does Éomer serve Éomund, Sauron, Saruman or Théoden?

31. Do hobbits learn to cook before they learn to read?

32. What is the Entwash: a lake, a sandy plain, a river or a forest?

33. Anborn is an elf, a man of Númenor, a rider of Rohan or a Black Rider?

34. What city is also known as the Dead City?

35. Who arranges to meet the Lord of the Mark and the others at Helm's Gate?

36. Who took the glass ball from Gandalf whilst he was sleeping?

37. Which direction do Faramir and his men face for a moment before eating a meal?

38. Eorl the Young brought the Rohan peoples, the ent peoples or the wood-elves out of the North in ancient times?

39. Into what part of Sam's body did Gollum sink his teeth?

40. What item does Frodo use to light the way in Shelob's Lair?

41. Sam cries when Frodo tells him that he doubts they will return from the Cracks of Doom: true or false?

42. How many men does Faramir leave to guard Sam and Frodo?

43. Gandalf knew all about Sam accompanying Frodo on his quest: true or false?

44. Which member of the Company first talked to the riders of Rohan?

45. Who does Gandalf urge Théoden to send to the mountains for safety?

46. How many men entered the ferns having seen Sam's cooking fire?

47. Were the orcs allowed to search their hobbit prisoners?

48. Who beheaded two orcs to save Éomer from an ambush?

49. What is the name of the Rohan horse only meant to be ridden by the Lord of the Mark?

50. Does Gandalf suggest to Saruman that he should have been a juggler, a jester, or a blacksmith to earn his keep?

Questions about The Return of the King

1. With which other hobbit does Bilbo set off to the Havens?

2. Is Umbar to the north, south, east or west of Minas Tirith?

3. How many feet long was the battering ram used to break open the gate at Minas Tirith?

4. The group of ruffians beside The Green Dragon inn were orcs, dwarves or men?

5. By what name do the men of Minas Tirith first call Gandalf?

6. Snaga quarrelled and fought with which orc captain as Sam watched?

7. Which hobbit married Rosie Cotton in the Spring of 1420?

8. How is Merry concealed to travel with the riders of Rohan to war?

9. What place, beginning with the letter O, was once the chief city of Gondor?

10. What happened to Merry's sword after he had struck the Lord of the Nazgûl?

11. By what word, beginning with the letter T, did Frodo, Sam, Pippin and Merry become known as in the Shire?

12. Who, Gandalf tells Pippin, can claim the kingship of Gondor if he comes?

13. Is Frodo wearing robes, his old clothes, a suit of armour or no clothes at all when Sam finds him in the Tower?

14. Who out of Imrahil, Aragorn and Éomer chose not to enter Minas Tirith immediately?

15. Who told Gandalf and Pippin at Minas Tirith of his encounters with Frodo and Sam?

16. How many arrows struck the leader of the ruffians as he attempted to hit Merry?

17. What part of Merry's body went numb after his attack on the Lord of the Nazgûl?

18. In which land would the New Year always start on the day that Sauron fell?

19. What is the name of the Minas Tirith dweller sent to Pippin to teach him some pass-words?

20. Lady Galadriel arrived at Minas Tirith on a white horse: true or false?

21. The road in Minas Tirith, called Rath Dinen, is known by what other name?

22. What happened to the gate arch after Sam and Frodo passed through it?

23. Who did Théoden hail as King of the Rohan before he died?

24. Which one of the following does not have a flaming beacon: Erelas, Nardol, Rivendell, Calenhad?

25. Using a hidden knife, Wormtongue cut whose throat?

26. Whose possessions did Sauron's soldiers show to Gandalf and the others?

27. The lands of Belfalas are ruled by which Prince, beginning with the letter I?

28. Who sat for days beside Faramir while the siege of Minas Tirith was under way?

29. Morthond Vale was in Rivendell, behind the Dark Door or in Eriador?

30. Sam wore only two items as a disguise in the Tower; one was a helmet, what was the other?

31. Was the first council after the Battle of Pelennor Fields held inside or outside the walls of Minas Tirith?

32. What is the name of Sam's first child: Frodo, Elanor, Erasmus or Galadriel?

33. What item of his disguise in Mordor did Frodo first discard?

34. The Stone of Erech was the height of a hobbit, the height of a man or the height of two men?

35. Does Legolas visit the Glittering Caves with Gimli?

36. Duilin and Derufin were the sons of Golasgil, Denethor, Duinhir or Imrahil?

37. The hands of a rightful king of which land can heal?

38. Who killed Lotho Sackville-Baggins while he slept?

39. What is the name of the rider of Rohan who hides Merry?

40. Which hobbits are forced to join in an orc march?

41. How many walls does the place known as the Guarded City have: three, five, seven or nine?

42. Narchost and Carchost are the names of which two towers in Mordor?

43. Which member of the Company of the Ring actually led the ships to Minas Tirith?

44. Which close friend of Frodo and the others was found in the Lockholes in the Shire?

45. What did Sam use to get past the Two Watchers?

46. Peregrin son of Paladin is the name Denethor gives which member of the Company of the Ring?

47. The Mouth of Sauron was a messenger on a horse, a statue or an enchanted stone?

48. Which two hobbits grew taller due to drinking ent-draughts?

49. After Sauron's defeat, who does Frodo leave Minas Tirith to see?

50. What was the colour of the sails of the ships that travelled to Minas Tirith?

QUIZ 2

1. Denethor showed Gandalf and Pippin what possession of Boromir's?

2. Who told tales and news to Saruman while he was still trapped in Orthanc tower?

3. What was the name of Merry's pony, on which he rode with Théoden?

4. Hob Hayward is recognised by which of the four hobbits?

5. Rath Celerdain is the Lampwrights', Blacksmiths' or Wheelwrights' Street?

6. Who vanished from the gate at Minas Tirith as the Rohan charged?

7. The old storage tunnels at Michel Delving have been turned into what?

8. Was Éowyn's shield arm or sword arm broken in the battle at Pelennor Fields?

9. How many tens of fathoms high was the White Tower at Minas Tirith?

10. Who does Sam see when he searches for water at night in Mordor?

11. How does Denethor plan for he and Faramir to die?

12. Pippin's new clothes at Minas Tirith were all green, all black and silver or all red and blue?

13. Which hobbit was hit violently in the back as he stood looking at the Cracks of Doom?

14. Whose words does Aragorn quote about the Paths of the Dead: Malbeth the Seer, Gregor the Sage or Wheeler the Wise?

15. To whom did Merry give some pipeweed out of pity?

16. Who was the second character that Pippin took to the Houses of Healing?

17. How old is Pippin when he reaches Minas Tirith?

18. Who did Aragorn ask for to bring his crown to him: Éowyn, Frodo or Treebeard?

19. Five miles past which ruined city did the forces leaving Minas Tirith rest after their first day's journey?

20. Which hobbit does Théoden release from his service and insist cannot come and fight with him?

21. Is Rosie Cotton from the Shire, Gondor or Mordor?

22. Which city did Aragorn see as under threat after looking into the Stone of Orthanc?

23. On what type of bird does Gandalf ride through Mordor to reach the Mountain of Doom?

24. What colour were the robes of the Guards of the gate to the Citadel at Minas Tirith?

25. Lockholes are safes, secret doors or prisons?

26. Were four, fourteen or twenty-four strokes of the battering ram required before the gates of Gondor broke open?

27. Which hobbit received a horn made of silver with an engraving of a horseman?

28. Golasgil was the lord of peoples from Pinnath Gelin, the Anfalas or Morthond?

29. When Sam and Frodo leapt off the path after escaping from the Tower, what did they land in?

30. What colour was the pony on which Merry rode with Théoden?

31. What colour was the cloth that covered the dead body of Théoden?

32. In which season did the household of Rivendell arrive at Minas Tirith?

33. Who locks eyes with Sauron's messenger, who appears from the Black Gate?

34. How many men in total did Pippin and Bergil watch enter Minas Tirith: fewer than 1000, fewer than 2000, fewer than 3000 or fewer than 5000?

35. Through what did Sam and Frodo enter the Mountain of Doom?

36. Who killed the chieftain of the Haradrim at Pelennor fields?

37. How many days did Théoden tell Aragorn it would take for them to ride to Dunharrow?

38. Was Breghelm, Vonhelm or Elfhelm in charge of the group of Rohan containing Dernhelm and Merry?

39. Who was invited to Aragorn's wedding but couldn't attend as there was too much to do in Rivendell?

40. Who does Merry cheekily ask to fetch him some pipeweed shortly after waking in the Houses of Healing?

41. Is Beregond a captain, a lord or a guard at Minas Tirith?

42. In what house in Hobbiton do the hobbits encounter Sharkey?

43. Who was the last creature to hold the ring before it fell into the Cracks of Doom?

44. Aragorn declared the oath of the Dead fulfilled once they arrived at Minas Tirith: true or false?

45. Which of the following men of Bree did not fight on the enemy's side: Harry Goatleaf, Tom Pickthorn or Bill Ferny?

46. What colour was the giant standard that Halbarad unfurled to show to the Dead?

47. Who, looking like a beggar, did the company come across on their journey to Rivendell?

48. Tom Cotton reckons there are fewer than 300, around 500 or more than 700 ruffians now living in the Shire?

49. Which two towers fell and were destroyed after the ring fell into the Cracks of Doom?

50. Who stands between Théoden and the Lord of the Nazgûl to protect Théoden?

QUIZ 3

1. Is Halbarad Dúnadan a ringwraith, a ranger, a lord of Gondor or a rider of Rohan?

2. Who was the first person Sam spoke to when waking up after the adventures at the Cracks of Doom?

3. How many men from Lossarnach did Bergil say they had hoped would arrive at Minas Tirith: 500, 2000, 5000 or 10,000?

4. What was the name given to the battle in the Shire, won by the hobbits?

5. Which friend of Pippin fell under a blow from a troll?

6. What is the colour of the staff with the golden knob that Denethor holds?

7. Sam found the dead bodies of what creature a short distance past the Two Watchers?

8. No hobbit has ever killed another on purpose in the Shire: true or false?

9. Whose mace shattered Lady Éowyn's shield?

10. How many hundreds of men of arms did Prince Imrahil bring with him to Minas Tirith?

11. What was the name, beginning with the letter A, of the Lord of Lamedon?

12. Who had taken and worn the orc mail shirt that Frodo discarded?

13. How many thousands of soldiers does Théoden estimate he can take to Minas Tirith?

14. Which one of the following is not a Lord of the Mark: Eorl the Young, Bergil, Aldor or Thengel?

15. Who is the first to realise that Lady Éowyn is not dead after her battle with the Lord of the Nazgûl?

16. Gandalf says he vouches for Pippin before the seat of which leader at Minas Tirith?

17. Which Tom does Gandalf say he plans to have a long talk with after leaving the hobbits?

18. Was Elfhelm, Éomer or Grimbold's company the first to attack the enemy's siege engines?

19. What was the name of the road Sam spotted on the Mountain of Doom?

20. Who is arrested by the Shire's Shirriffs for breaking many rules including bribing guards with food?

21. Which member of the Company do Legolas and Gimli accompany after they leave Théoden and Merry?

22. Does Imrahil, Aragorn or Gimli despair of the small force leaving Minas Tirith to fight the enemy?

23. How many leagues away from Isengard is Minas Tirith: 50, 100, 150 or 250?

24. Which of the following did not perish at Pelennor fields: Forlong, Imrahil or Halbarad?

25. Who asks Théoden and Éomer about the Paths of the Dead?

26. Which creatures held the old castle of Durthang that Sam and Frodo viewed?

27. Who, at Minas Tirith, does Pippin think has gone insane?

28. Sam rode to which household to raise the hobbits to defend the Shire?

29. Which member of the Company of the Ring believed Minas Tirith needed more gardens?

30. The Púkel-men were Sauron's guards, giants from Fangorn or statues of stone?

31. Slaves were used to row the ships of Umbar: true or false?

32. How many riders accompanied Halbarad Dúnadan when he meets the Company of the Ring: 10, 20, 30, 40 or 50?

33. Who stabbed the Lord of the Nazgûl in the back of his knee?

34. Saruman is never released from the tower of Orthanc: true or false?

35. Who bit Frodo with his fangs beside the Cracks of Doom?

36. What red item does the messenger bring to Théoden from Denethor?

37. The Mouth of Sauron lists many demands in return for who or what?

38. Which member of the company does Legolas call Master Sluggard?

39. By what name does Lotho insist those of the Shire call him?

40. Ioreth was the youngest, eldest or most beautiful of the women who served in the Houses of Healing?

41. How many levels is Minas Tirith built on?

42. Orcs have fangs: true or false?

43. Who does Beregond say can see into the future?

44. The Tooks, the Brandybucks or the Cottons were the first to shoot at the ruffians?

45. What was the name given to the sickness that came from the Nazgûl?

46. Several companies of orc jostling to complete their march allowed Frodo and Sam to escape: true or false?

47. There are rumours of a great fleet coming to attack allies of Gondor from Umbar, Mordor, Eriador or Rohan?

48. Which messenger from Gondor did the Rohan believe they had found dead and beheaded?

49. How many hobbits were killed in the Battle of Bywater: none, 19, 39 or 59?

50. Who leaves Silent Street to search for Gandalf in order to save Faramir?

QUIZ 4

1. Théoden makes which member of the Company his partner on the ride to Dunharrow?

2. Gléowine was a minstrel, a soldier, or a healer?

3. What colour was the Stone of Erech?

4. What inn on the edge of the Shire has been torn down?

5. What was the name of the tomb in which Denethor and Faramir lay?

6. By what other name is the mountain called Dwimorberg known?

7. Pelargir was 22, 32, 42 or 52 leagues away from Harlond, the closest harbour point to Minas Tirith?

8. The Mountain of Doom lies in the middle of which plains, beginning with the letter G?

9. Who gives Merry a leather jerkin, shield and knife to protect him?

10. Who carried the injured Faramir to the White Tower?

11. Mr Butterbur warns Gandalf and the hobbits of strange goings-on in what part of Middle-earth apart from Bree?

12. Which of the patients is allowed to leave the Houses of Healing first?

13. For how many hours was Pippin first questioned by Denethor?

14. What does Denethor plan to use along with wood to make a funeral pyre?

15. How many hundreds of men from Lossarnach did Bergil and Pippin watch enter Minas Tirith?

16. Who did Pippin share a room with for his first night at Minas Tirith?

17. Who beheaded the Lord of the Nazgûl's mount with a single sword stroke?

18. Who has, and shows Aragorn, the keys to the tower of Orthanc: Gandalf, Quickbeam or Treebeard?

19. Who leaps on Frodo shortly before they reach the Cracks of Doom?

20. The Lord of the Nazgûl killed whose horse?

21. What was Aragorn's name when he became king?

22. Who did Beregond and Gandalf carry out of the tombs at Minas Tirith?

23. How many of the Company of the Ring left Isengard led by Aragorn?

24. Where did the forces of Umbar and Harad flee on seeing the dead arrive with Aragorn's company: Linhir, Erech or Fornost?

25. Who did King Elessar appoint as captain of the White Guard?

26. Who did Aragorn heal first: Merry, Faramir or Lady Éowyn?

27. Where was Lobelia Sackville-Baggins taken to by the ruffians?

28. What was the chilling name of the paths along which Aragorn chooses to ride?

29. All the inns of the Shire were closed whilst the hobbits were away: true or false?

30. Which of the following items does Frodo not wear as a disguise: a green cape, a black cap, a leather tunic and hairy breeches?

31. Who awakes after Aragorn bathes her forehead and arm with leaves and water?

32. Was Gimli, Aragorn, Legolas or Halbarad the last member of the Company to go through the Dark Door?

33. Hob Hayward receives his orders from which relative of Bilbo's?

34. How were the 500 men that arrived with Duinhuir at Minas Tirith armed?

35. What did Merry first ask for when he awoke from Aragorn's healing?

36. Who actually crowned Aragorn at Minas Tirith?

37. What is the name of the great spiked gate that bars the hobbits' way back over the Brandywine?

38. Which one of the following did not perish at Pelennor fields: Grimbold, Beregond or Hirluin the fair?

39. Who, beginning with the letter I, was believed to have set the Stone of Erech in its current resting place?

40. The Second Age, Third Age or Fourth Age finished with Sauron being defeated?

41. Who fought and killed several of Denethor's guards to prevent him killing Faramir?

42. Which is the furthest away from Minas Tirith: Lebennin, Tumladen or Lossarnach?

43. Which hobbit removes all of his orc clothing first?

44. Who told Sam that Bill the pony had arrived back safely in Bree?

45. Which member of the Grey Company did not fear the ghosts of men?

46. The ships first thought to be the Corsairs of Umbar arrived at Minas Tirith on what river?

47. Which of the four hobbits did not force the men to flee along the Hobbiton Road?

48. Meneldor, Landroval and Gwaihir rescued which two characters?

49. How many soldiers on foot marched out of Minas Tirith a few days after the Battle of the Pelennor Fields?

50. With what drink did Pippin wash down his first breakfast at Minas Tirith with Beregond?

QUIZ 5

1. Who said goodbye and left the hobbits first: Gimli, Aragorn or Gandalf?

2. In what month was the Battle of the Pelennor Fields?

3. Denethor's father was Théoden, Ecthelion or Vorondil?

4. How many hills near the Black Gate do the forces from Minas Tirith arrange themselves around to face the forces of Mordor?

5. Bilbo gave Merry and Pippin a gift before they parted: what was it?

6. An orc shot an arrow and hit Gollum in the back from 30, 40, 50 or 60 paces?

7. What is the name of Beregond's son who befriends Pippin?

8. Who reveals to Gandalf and Pippin that he has a palantír to see with?

9. Who does Bilbo ask to take his papers, notes and diary back to the Shire?

10. Who declares he will not fulfil his deed at the Cracks of Doom?

11. Guthláf was banner-bearer to which leader of the Rohan?

12. Who does Halbarad Dúnadan say he and his group are searching for?

13. What was the name of the houses where Faramir was taken by Pippin and Beregond?

14. The owner of which inn is amazed to find that the new King was Strider the Ranger?

15. Were the mines and forges of Mordor in the North or the South?

16. Which leader, the father of Boromir, do Gandalf and Pippin meet at Minas Tirith?

17. Sam carried Frodo on his back half the way, a quarter of the way or all the way up the Mountain of Doom in one go?

18. Frodo and the others spent their second night back in the Shire in Frogmorton, Hobbiton or Michel Delving?

19. Who did Dervorin lead into Minas Tirith: the men of Ringló Vale, Ethir, or Blackfoot Vale?

20. Who, of the following, was not looked after at the Houses of Healing: Merry, Imrahil, Faramir or Lady Éowyn?

21. Whose 129th birthday celebrations do the hobbits and Gandalf attend?

22. Which leader of Gondor tells Lady Éowyn that she is beautiful?

23. Who had a hill pony arranged for Merry so that the hobbit could ride with him?

24. Whose father was turned out of his house on Bagshot Row?

25. To lighten their load, Sam and Frodo discard the sword, Sting: true or false?

26. Who goes to defend the Pelennor defences manned by Faramir?

27. 25th March was the date that Sauron fell, that Théoden died or that Aragorn first arrived at Minas Tirith?

28. Faramir was brought back from battle on Gandalf's horse: true or false?

29. On both banks of what river does the ruined city of Osgiliath stand?

30. Which member of the Company saved Pippin, who was buried underneath a troll?

31. Kingsfoil is: a king's crown, Théoden's servant, a healing herb or a sleeping potion?

32. Who does Frodo just manage to stop slaying Saruman in Hobbiton?

33. Did King Elessar pardon, imprison or execute the easterlings who gave themselves up?

34. The door called Fen Hollen is in the second, third, fifth or sixth wall of Minas Tirith?

35. Did Pippin consider Minas Tirith to be more or less beautiful than Isengard?

36. What creatures' clothes does Frodo put on to disguise himself?

37. Who buries his quarrel with Éomer after Sauron has been defeated?

38. Dol Amroth is the name of whose castle: Aragorn's, Denethor's, Lady Celeborn's or Prince Imrahil's?

39. Bywater is where the Shirriffs have been told to take the four hobbits: true or false?

40. Who sang the tale of Frodo of the Nine Fingers and the Ring of Doom?

41. What is Dernhelm's true identity, revealed to the Lord of the Nazgûl?

42. Which hobbit swears to serve the leader of Minas Tirith?

43. Sam and Frodo overhear two orcs saying who has spoiled the tracking scent?

44. What sort of heirloom did Éowyn give to one of the hobbits?

45. Who volunteers to lead forces to defend the Anduin River?

46. Southrons and easterlings were on the side of the Rohan or the enemy at Pelennor?

47. Which chapter of Frodo's book is left unfinished for Sam to complete: chapter 30, chapter 40, chapter 60 or chapter 80?

48. Sammath Naur is also known as the Chambers of Light, Chambers of Fire or Chambers of Living Death?

49. Who killed a great troll-chief which then fell on top of him?

50. Who did Gandalf disarm in Minas Tirith by raising his hand?

QUIZ 6

1. What is the name, beginning with the letter F, of the Lord of Lossarnach?

2. Who alone stood to confront the Lord of the Nazgûl as he entered Minas Tirith?

3. Who commanded Pippin to go to the Citadel of Minas Tirith to be given new clothes?

4. What road runs from Barad-dûr to the Chambers of Fire?

5. To which one of the hobbits did Bilbo give a small bag of gold?

6. Which hobbit was the first to set eyes on the Mountain of Fire?

7. What was the name of the woman who married Aragorn?

8. Which hobbit is Gandalf carrying as a passenger on his horse at the very start of the book?

9. What item of Frodo's clothing started the quarrel between Gorbag and Shagrat?

10. Windfola was the Rohan horse of Isildur, Dernholm or Éomer?

11. The hobbits had met Sharkey before, but by what name did they know him?

12. Who wears a Lórien grey cloak to enter Minas Tirith alongside Gandalf?

13. What colour was the glare that came from the Cracks of Doom?

14. Who gives Frodo an item of jewellery to protect him from memories of fear?

15. Which group of forest dwellers used poisoned arrows and offered their service to Théoden?

16. How many gates are there at Minas Tirith?

17. With what weapon did Saruman attempt to kill Frodo in the Shire?

18. Who was the first orc Sam heard speak after reaching the top tier of the tower?

19. Men wearing the white symbol of a tree, silver crown and stars hail from Eriador, Gondor, Rohan or the Shire?

20. Did the fleet of Umbar comprise 30, 50, 80 or 100 great ships?

21. Which father gave away his daughter for Aragorn to marry?

22. Carach Angren is the Isenmouthe, the Anduinmouthe or the Breemouthe?

23. The Lord of the Nazgûl was the first member of the enemy to walk into Minas Tirith: true or false?

24. Elladan and Elohir rode with Halbarad Dúnadan when they met the Company: true or false?

25. Who became prince of Ithilien after Sauron was defeated?

26. Which one of the following places does not have a flaming beacon: Amon Dîn, Mindolluin, Eilenach, Halifirien?

27. Who turned out to be Lotho Sackville-Baggins' 'Big Man'?

28. Does Denethor, Faramir or Beregond refer to Frodo as a witless Halfling?

29. Who becomes King of Gondor and Lord of the Western Lands?

30. Who does Éomer announce will marry Faramir?

31. Gorbag injured Shagrat with a punch, a knife wound or by breaking his leg?

32. The enemy used catapults to launch firebombs into Minas Tirith: true or false?

33. No horse is allowed into the Citadel at Minas Tirith: true or false?

34. Which hobbit was allowed to go with the force leaving Minas Tirith?

35. What was the last word that was heard from Gollum as he fell into the Cracks of Doom?

36. What was the name of the messenger who brought a message to Théoden from Denethor?

37. Snaga reached the chamber containing Frodo with a ladder, a rope or a bridge?

38. Théoden is killed by an orc arrow at Pelennor fields: true or false?

39. Which White Rider scattered the five Black Riders in front of Minas Tirith?

40. How many days prior to his meeting with Gandalf and Pippin did Denethor hear Boromir's horn sound?

41. Snaga fell to his death, was killed by Shagrat or was killed by Sam?

42. Sharkey is alleged to be in charge of Rivendell, the Shire, Bree or Mordor?

43. What is the name, beginning with the letter N, given to the meal taken at Minas Tirith at midday or shortly after?

44. Landroval is an orc, a lord of Gondor, an elf or an eagle?

45. Grond was the name of a leader of the Orcs, a battering ram or Sauron's sword?

46. To whom does Bilbo give three books of lore he had written?

47. For how many days does Aragorn advise that Lady Éowyn rest at the Houses of Healing?

48. How many swift streams does the land of Lebennin, south of Minas Tirith have?

49. As a punishment for calling out, Snaga hit Frodo with what weapon?

50. What was the name of the great battle fought by the Rohan in view of Minas Tirith?

QUIZ 7

1. Púkel-men could be found in Rohan, Mordor, the Shire or Eriador?

2. Who grabs the hobbits' possessions, shown by Sauron's messenger?

3. Which two hobbits were made knights of the City and of the Mark?

4. What is the name, beginning with the letter W, of the Wild Men of the Woods?

5. Frodo became Mayor, Deputy Mayor or Head Shirriff whilst Old Will Whitfoot recovered from being imprisoned?

6. Who heard what he thought was the orcs, Shagrat and Gorbag, fighting?

7. Mindoullin is a mountain in Gondor, Mordor, Rohan or Eriador?

8. Hill-trolls, orcs or ringwraiths were the first to attack Gandalf and the others?

9. Who sang a song to Arod the horse to make him pass through the Dark Door?

10. How many heads did each of the Two Watchers have?

11. What word, beginning with the letter G, do Woses use as a name for orc-folk?

12. Rammas Echor is a lake, a hill, a wall or a forest?

13. Who does Faramir declare his love for?

14. Snowbourn is: a mountain, a river, a citadel or a hill range?

15. Lobelia Sackville-Baggins left all her money to which hobbit to use to rebuild homes?

16. Pippin had been at Minas Tirith for less than a week, one and a half weeks or three weeks before the city was besieged?

17. Is Frodo angry and rude, tired and in pain or happy and joking moments after Sam returns the ring to him?

18. Was leechcraft, witchcraft or medical chanting used to help heal injured people in Minas Tirith?

19. Into which house did Sam and his wife move?

20. How many leagues from Minas Tirith was the place where Faramir and Frodo parted?

21. How many hours does Éomer reckon it will take for Ghân-buri-Ghân to lead the first Rohan to Minas Tirith?

22. How many days before Bilbo's next birthday do the hobbits and Gandalf arrive at Rivendell?

23. Which enemy fleet lay mainly at Pelargir?

24. Whose father farms lands near Tuckborough in the Shire?

25. What part of Frodo's body was bitten and injured by Gollum?

26. Ghân-buri-Ghân is a headman of the Woses, orcs or the men of Gondor?

27. Who called out to the Dead, calling them Oathbreakers?

28. Why does Sam want to drink from the stream in Mordor first?

29. Gandalf led the army leaving Minas Tirith: true or false?

30. What is the name of the first guard to speak to Gandalf at Minas Tirith?

31. Gandalf accompanies the hobbits back home to the Shire: true or false?

32. The Two Watchers prevented which hobbit from entering the tower?

33. Denethor set his own funeral pyre alight to burn himself: true or false?

34. What are the two words, beginning with R and with E, which form the name of the outer wall that protects Minas Tirith?

35. Aragorn set up camp outside Minas Tirith in a tent, a hut, a cave or a trench?

36. What sort of creature first brought news of victory to Gondor: a horse, an eagle or an elf?

37. Roheryn was the name of whose horse?

38. What item did Gandalf and Aragorn bring back to Minas Tirith?

39. Angbor is expected to arrive at Minas Tirith with how many thousand men?

40. Forlong is known by what overweight nickname?

41. Which non-hobbit member of the Company of the Ring travelled to the Havens?

42. What did the enemy fire into Minas Tirith after the firebombs?

43. Which of the following is not a member of the Cotton family: Rosie, Nibs, Dabs or Jolly?

44. What land's beacons, when lit, are a call for aid, according to Gandalf?

45. Sam's first swipe with his sword removed what part of Snaga's body?

46. The Grey Company led by Aragorn visited which Lady at Dunharrow?

47. In the shape of what creature's head was the head of the battering ram used at Minas Tirith?

48. Which hobbit was sent to Faramir to talk of the Lady Éowyn?

49. How many leaves of kingsfoil did Bergil bring to Aragorn?

50. Who pleads with Aragorn to be allowed to join his quest on the Paths of the Dead?

The Fellowship of the Ring Answers

1. White
2. Baggins
3. A three-storey building
4. East
5. Goldberry
6. Two
7. Sam
8. Mushrooms
9. Green and yellow
10. Elrond

11. True
12. Three
13. Glóin
14. They had vanished
15. Frodo
16. Hobbits
17: Proudfoot
18. Forest
19. Wizard
20. A Great Eagle

21. He puts on the ring
22. Stream
23. Athelas
24. Merry Brandybuck
25. Mr Butterbur

26. Boat
27. Seven
28. Sauron's
29. Twice
30. Breeds of hobbit

31. Mr Maggot
32. Over 250 years old
33. Frodo
34. Lord Celeborn
35. Ringwraiths
36. A pen
37. Strider
38. Ham Gamgee
39. Pippin
40. Sam

41. Merry
42. The River Withywindle
43. Gandalf
44. An empty bookcase
45. Paddles
46. Fallohides
47. Orcs
48. Sam
49. Writing a book
50. A sword

QUIZ 2

1. Aragorn
2. A log
3. Inglorion
4. Flick-tail
5. Michel Delving
6. Legolas
7. A rope ladder
8. Green
9. Ori
10. Mountain

11. The points of the compass
12. Crows
13. Balin's
14. Sam and Pippin
15. Three
16. The Dark Lord
17. One hour
18. A sword
19. Waymoot
20. 100 years

21. Gandalf
22. Boromir
23. The White Council
24. A lake
25. Four
26. Frodo
27. One

28. Rangers
29. Sackville-Baggins
30. It broke and fell out of his hand

31. The Argonath or The Pillars of the Kings
32. Bilbo and Frodo
33. Lobelia Sackville-Baggins
34. The crystal phial
35. The Master-ring
36. Hobbiton
37. 60
38. Saruman
39. A watch-tower
40. Six

41. The Golden Perch
42. Gil-galad
43. On foot
44. The Hall of Fire
45. Three
46. Gandalf the Grey
47. Crickhollow
48. Mushrooms
49. Bree-land
50. Merry and Pippin

QUIZ 3

1. White
2. Frodo
3. True
4. The Gaffer
5. A beard
6. His staff
7. Bilbo
8. The Ford of Rivendell
9. Harry
10. Brandy Hall

11. Gollum
12. Tobleycold
13. Sam Gamgee
14. Two
15. Aragorn
16. Gold
17. True
18. Do not travel by night
19. Mr Maggot
20. Rivendell

21. Elves
22. True
23. A long dagger
24. Gimli
25. Glóin

26. Little Folk
27. Gollum
28. Moria-silver or true-silver
29. The Mountain of Fire
30. An ancient tower

31. Brandybuck
32. Seven years
33. Merry
34. Tower
35. A mountain
36. Hobbits
37. His shoulder
38. True
39. Harfoots
40. False

41. White
42. Barrows
43. Bilbo Baggins
44. Bilbo
45. Otho
46. 12 silver pennies
47. A great huntsman
48. Bilbo
49. Eight
50. Buckleberry

QUIZ 4

1. Frodo Baggins
2. A spear
3. Five
4. Frodo
5. Tom Bombadil
6. Lothlórien (Golden Wood)
7. Friend
8. The Old Forest
9. Midgewater Marshes
10. Sam

11. October
12. Gandalf
13. An orc
14. Black Riders
15. A bird
16. All
17. Burn
18. Shadowfax
19. Dwarves
20. Frodo

21. Orodruin
22. Bilbo Baggins
23. Moria
24. Celeborn

25. Firewood
26. North
27. The ring
28. A dragon
29. The River Hoarwell
30. Gimli

31. Black Riders
32. By drowning
33. Tom Bombadil's
34. Saruman the White
35. 33
36. Yellow
37. A valuable metal
38. Strider
39. Fatty
40. Citadel of the Stars

41. The Great River
42. Sam Gamgee
43. An axe
44. Boats
45. Six
46. Orcs
47. Pipe-weed
48. Fatty Bolger
49. Redhorn
50. Balin's

QUIZ 5

1. Mr Butterbur
2. Threw it into the fire
3. Gandalf
4. Tom Bombadil
5. Dora Baggins
6. Holly trees
7. Elladan and Elrohir
8. Gandalf
9. Tom Bombadil
10. Sam Gamgee

11. Bilbo's speech
12. Three
13. Mordor
14. A wraith under the control of the Dark Lord
15. The Dark Lord
16. True
17. Dinner or supper
18. Elves
19. The Black Breath
20. September

21. Strider
22. Water lilies
23. Four
24. Rangers
25. Dwarves

26. The Dark Tower
27. Thingol
28. Legolas
29. Frodo
30. A dragon
31. Mithril (or Moria-silver)
32. The Dark Lord
33. A shirt of mail
34. Riddles
35. Elf
36. 99
37. Lady Galadriel
38. Orcs
39. A Black Rider
40. They give presents

41. True
42. Red wine
43. Fire
44. Boffin
45. A staff
46. A knife
47. A brooch
48. Seven
49. Elves
50. False

QUIZ 6

1. No
2. Gandalf
3. One
4. The Council of Elrond
5. A dwarf
6. A brooch
7. The Mayor of Michel Delving
8. Eleven
9. Mother
10. Taller

11. Saruman
12. Legolas
13. Horses
14. The Mirror of Galadriel
15. The Seat of Seeing
16. The Doors of Durin
17. Strider
18. Three
19. A public house
20. 111

21. Three
22. Pippin
23. It shines
24. Elrond

25. Bilbo
26. Strider (Aragorn)
27. Three
28. Gollum
29. A museum
30. Sackville-Baggins

31. Grip
32. Larger
33. Gandalf
34. Drogo
35. Glorfindel
36. Three
37. Merry
38. The Cracks of Doom
39. Slippers
40. Strider

41. One
42. Aragorn
43. Aragorn
44. Bree
45. Fatty Lumpkin
46. Sam Gamgee
47. Friend
48. Fatty Bolger
49. Pippin
50. Drogo

QUIZ 7

1. Dwarves
2. A tentacle
3. A dwarf
4. Singing a song
5. Tom Bombadil
6. Merry
7. Nine
8. Gandalf
9. Silver
10. 40 years

11. Sam
12. None
13. False
14. A short sword
15. To travel with the hobbits
16. Dáin
17. 200
18. Bilbo
19. The Gamgees
20. A pale lake

21. Boromir
22. The Brandywine
23. Right
24. False
25. Three

26. A cloak (with a hood)
27. A mine
28. Dúnadan
29. Gandalf
30. A Balrog

31. The Prancing Pony
32. Elrond
33. Gollum
34. Weathertop hill
35. Boromir
36. Merry
37. December
38. Elrond
39. 1418
40. Gold chains

41. Old Man Willow
42. Glorfindel
43. Frodo
44. The Great River
45. An umbrella
46. A mathom
47. The Plough or Great Bear
48. Pippin
49. An axe
50. Legolas

QUIZ 8

1. The Prancing Pony inn
2. Friend
3. Minas Anor
4. Weathertop
5. A tree
6. Smaller
7. The Pillars of the Kings
8. An enchanted river
9. He vanished
10. Caras Galadhon

11. Goldberry
12. Holes in the ground
13. Trees
14. Harfoots
15 Aragorn (Strider)
16. Bree
17. Mr Maggot
18. Seven
19. 100
20. Axes

21. True
22. Merry
23. Aragorn (Strider)
24. Sam

25. Sauron, The Dark Lord
26. False
27. Gandalf
28. 144
29. Fatty Bolger
30. Fog

31. Isildur Elendil
32. Opponents
33. Mr Mugwort
34. A sword
35. Boromir
36. Eight
37. Elrond
38. Mr Underhill
39. Shirriffs
40. Orcs

41. In a barrow
42. Gandalf's
43. Déagol
44. Boromir
45. White
46. Gandalf
47. The Old Forest
48. True
49. Eregion
50. The Prancing Pony

QUIZ 9

1. A hill
2. Bill Ferny
3. The Misty Mountains
4. Harfoots
5. White wolves
6. Three
7. Lothlórien
8. The ring
9. 10 o'clock
10. Gandalf

11. Merry
12. Lobelia Sackville-Baggins
13. Green
14. Hobbiton
15. Three
16. Rope
17. True
18. Bilbo Baggins
19. The ring
20. An elf

21. One
22. Elwing
23. Rohan
24. False
25. 20-33

26. Ablaze with fire
27. Boromir
28. Fish
29. A river
30. Gimli

31. Three
32. Frodo's
33. Pippin
34. Goldberry
35. He returned to the Shire
36. Rauros-foot
37. Around his neck
38. The Gamgees'
39. The Shire
40. Bill Ferny

41. Elves
42. Fallohide
43. The Redhorn
44. Her uncle
45. The Prancing Pony
46. A mountain
47. True
48. Sam Gamgee
49. The Brandywine
50. Woodlands

The Two Towers Answers

QUIZ 1

1. Wormtongue
2. His wooden staff
3. Éowyn
4. Legolas and Gimli
5. Minas Tirith
6. Entmoot
7. Goblin-soldiers
8. Quickbeam
9. Third
10. Ankles

11. Gúthwinē
12. Brown Lands
13. Dawn
14. Thirty
15. An elf
16. Lembas
17. A tree
18. Sam
19. Gandalf
20. The Winding Stair

21. Pippin
22. Ents
23. Wormtongue
24. Gollum
25. The Horn of Boromir
26. White

27. Saruman
28. West
29. Stronger
30. Eats the meat of living creatures

31. Gollum
32. Boromir
33. Sam Gamgee
34. A cloth
35. Orcs
36. Sunrise
37. Merry and Pippin
38. Orcs
39. Through a tunnel
40. Saruman's

41. Sam
42. They were burned
43. Fangorn
44. True
45. Pillar of the White Hand
46. His eyes stay open
47. An eye
48. Arrows
49. Shelob's
50. Yes

138

QUIZ 2

1. The Orthanc-stone
2. Merry
3. It broke
4. Heavy axes
5. Untied itself
6. Merry
7. One
8. The Ringwraiths
9. Théoden
10. A sacred horse

11. Gondor
12. Fimbrethil
13. Théoden
14. The Nazgûl
15. Pippin's
16. He died
17. True
18. Orcs
19. Gondor
20. Valley of Saruman

21. 24
22. 12th Steward
23. Gandalf and the others found Merry and Pippin
24. The Valley of Living Death
25. Helm's Deep

26. Sam
27. Éomer
28. Watchwood
29. Hasufel
30. Ells

31. Elves
32. His sword
33. A mountain range
34. Oliphaunt
35. Treebeard
36. The phial of Galadriel
37. Erkenbrand
38. Crumbs and cut cords
39. Grishnákh
40. 30 ells

41. Two
42. Bands of gold
43. Entings
44. Minas Tirith
45. Horses
46. Quickbeam
47. True
48. Black
49. Éomer
50. True

QUIZ 3

1. Ithilien
2. Gandalf
3. Gollum
4. Gimli
5. Gollum
6. Gandalf
7. Seven
8. Háma
9. 26th Steward
10. By night

11. Gollum
12. Six
13. Gandalf Greyhame
14. Mordor
15. Mithrandir
16. Aragorn
17. Frodo
18. Orthanc
19. A knife
20. The Noldor

21. Gandalf
22. Legolas
23. The Dead Marshes
24. Orcs
25. True
26. Shadowfax

27. Saruman
28. Mordor
29. Aragorn
30. Faramir

31. False
32. Sting
33. Théoden
34. True
35. 1,000
36. Four
37. Gimli
38. The phial of Galadriel
39. Legolas
40. Three

41. Gandalf
42. Elves
43. A wooden staff
44. False
45. Ents
46. The candles of corpses
47. A battering ram
48. Treebeard's
49. Horse
50. Boromir

QUIZ 4

1. Bound in cords
2. Éomer
3. Osgiliath
4. Éomund
5. Men of Gondor
6. False
7. Beechbone
8. A forest
9. Isildur's Bane
10. Frodo

11. Isengarder orc
12. Its head
13. Lembas
14. False
15. Four
16. Aragorn
17. Erebor
18. The Tower of the Moon (Minas Ithil)
19. 41
20. Giant cobwebs

21. Two daggers
22. His sister
23. Eldeón
24. Elves
25. Alive

26. Legolas and Gimli
27. Sam
28. East
29. True
30. The boats

31. Sauron
32. Pepper
33. Nine
34. Ents
35. Lugbúrz
36. Rauros
37. Minas Morgul
38. 50
39. Bread
40. Gollum

41. Bregalad
42. True
43. Gimli
44. Two
45. The ents
46. 1000
47. Sam Gamgee
48. Parth Galen
49. Rabbit
50. Gandalf

QUIZ 5

1. 105
2. Dagorlad
3. The House of Eorl
4. True
5. False
6. Mordor
7. Éowyn
8. Faramir
9. The Entwash
10. Father of horses

11. Éored
12. Brother
13. False
14. A brooch
15. Beren
16. Gollum
17. Gimli's
18. Sam
19. He stood in the rain
20. Saruman

21. Boromir
22. Orcs
23. Swords
24. Saruman's
25. Palantíri
26. Frodo
27. Saruman

28. Helm's Deep
29. Lady Galadriel
30. Gandalf

31. One year and a day
32. Frodo
33. Once
34. Two
35. Orcs
36. An orc
37. The Orthanc-stone
38. Bay leaves, sage and thyme
39. Halflings
40. Frodo

41. Frodo's
42. The Misty Mountains
43. Aragorn
44. Isengard
45. The Mountains of Shadow
46. Wingfoot
47. Sam
48. Mordor
49. Fladrif
50. Gandalf

QUIZ 6

1. The phial of Galadriel
2. 70
3. Wormtongue
4. Minas Tirith
5. Frodo
6. Three
7. Emyn Muil
8. His horse
9. A waterfall
10. None

11. The foul smell
12. His ankle
13. Faramir
14. Treebeard
15. Mauhúr
16. To fight with Théoden and the others
17. An ent
18. One of her eyes
19. A large stone
20. Burnt them

21. True
22. Treebeard's
23. Gandalf
24. Blindfold them
25. Fangorn
26. Helm's Dike

27. A waterfall
28. Isengard
29. True
30. Fish

31. Lugdush
32. Snowbane
33. Théoden and Aragorn
34. Pippin and Merry
35. Lady Galadriel
36. Second Marshal of the Mark
37. 27
38. At night
39. True
40. Faramir

41. Théoden
42. Minas Morgul
43. Gríma
44. Sam Gamgee
45. His hand
46. The Key of Orthanc and Saruman's wizard's staff
47. Red
48. Gollum
49. Sauron
50. At least fourteen feet high

QUIZ 7

1. True
2. Green gauntlets and masks
3. Denuidin
4. Three weeks
5. Legolas
6. Six
7. Treebeard
8. 45 leagues
9. Twenty feet
10. One

11. Boromir's horn
12. Rope
13. Eating and drinking
14. Gwaihir the Windlord
15. Old Entish
16. Saruman
17. Pippin's
18. A whip
19. Marshes
20. Gimli

21. Whiteskins
22. Gimli
23. A strength-reviving bread
24. Saruman's
25. Isengard

26. Minas Tirith
27. His uncle
28. A tree stump
29. Fill pans with water
30. False

31. Sam
32. Aragorn, Legolas and Gimli
33. Two
34. The Men of Rohan
35. Frodo
36. The Shire
37. Death
38. Frodo
39. Two
40. In Shelob's lair

41. Nazgûl
42. He spat
43. False
44. Wormtongue
45. The Teeth of Mordor
46. A spear
47. Sting (Frodo's sword)
48. West
49. The Mountains of Shadow
50. Uglúk

QUIZ 8

1. The Valley of Living Death
2. The riders of Rohan
3. False
4. Pippin's
5. South
6. The Haunted Pass
7. Shelob
8. Screamed in pain
9. Uglúk
10. Saruman's staff

11. Éomer
12. Gimli
13. Wormtongue (Grima)
14. The Straight Stair
15. A curved scimitar
16. Isildur's Bane
17. Fewer than thirty
18. Éomer
19. Gandalf
20. Isengard

21. Isengarders
22. A shield
23. Anduin
24. The Isen
25. A staff

26. Treebeard
27. A boat
28. Rabbits
29. Sam
30. Théoden

31. Yes
32. A river
33. A man of Númenor
34. Minas Morgul
35. Gandalf
36. Pippin
37. West
38. The Rohan peoples
39. Sam's shoulder
40. The phial of Galadriel

41. True
42. Two
43. False
44. Aragorn
45. Women, children and the old
46. Four
47. No
48. Gimli
49. Shadowfax
50. A jester

The Return of the King Answers

1. Frodo
2. South
3. 100 feet
4. Men
5. Mithrandir
6. Shagrat
7. Sam
8. Under a rider's cloak
9. Osgiliath
10. It smoked and disappeared

11. The Travellers
12. Aragorn
13. No clothes at all
14. Aragorn
15. Faramir
16. Four
17. His right arm
18. Gondor
19. Beregond
20. True

21. Silent Street
22. It crumbled and fell
23. Éomer
24. Rivendell
25. Saruman's

26. Sam and Frodo's
27. Imrahil
28. Denethor
29. Behind the Dark Door
30. A black cloak

31. Outside
32. Elanor
33. The chain mail shirt
34. The height of a man
35. Yes
36. Duinhir
37. Gondor
38. Wormtongue
39. Dernhelm
40. Sam and Frodo

41. Seven
42. The Towers of the Teeth
43. Aragorn
44. Fredegar Bolger
45. The phial of Galadriel
46. Pippin
47. Messenger on a horse
48. Pippin and Merry
49. Bilbo
50. Black

QUIZ 2

1. His horn
2. Treebeard
3. Stybba
4. Merry
5. Old Lampwrights' Street
6. The Lord of the Nazgûl
7. Prisons
8. Her shield arm
9. Fifty
10. Gollum

11. By being burned alive
12. All black and silver
13. Sam
14. Malbeth the Seer
15. Saruman
16. Merry
17. 28
18. Frodo
19. Osgiliath
20. Merry

21. The Shire
22. Minas Tirith
23. An eagle
24. Black

25. Prisons
26. Four
27. Merry
28. The Anfalas
29. Thorn bushes
30. Grey

31. Gold
32. Summer
33. Aragorn
34. Fewer than 3000
35. A door
36. Théoden
37. Three
38. Elfhelm
39. Bilbo
40. Aragorn

41. A guard
42. Bag End
43. Gollum
44. False
45. Tom Pickthorn
46. Black
47. Saruman
48. Fewer than 300
49. The Towers of Teeth
50. Dernhelm

QUIZ 3

1. A Ranger
2. Gandalf
3. 2000
4. The Battle of Bywater
5. Beregond
6. White
7. Orcs
8. True
9. The Lord of the Nazgûl
10. Seven

11. Angbor
12. Gollum
13. Six
14. Bergil
15. Prince Imrahil
16. Denethor
17. Tom Bombadil
18. Elfhelm's
19. Sauron's Road
20. Frodo

21. Aragorn
22. Imrahil
23. 150
24. Imrahil
25. Merry

26. Orcs
27. Denethor
28. The Cottons
29. Legolas
30. Statues of stone

31. True
32. 30
33. Merry
34. False
35. Gollum
36. The Red Arrow
37. The Hobbits (Frodo and Sam)
38. Merry
39. The Chief
40. Eldest

41. Seven
42. True
43. Denethor
44. The Tooks
45. The Black Shadow
46. True
47. Umbar
48. Hirgon
49. 19
50. Pippin

QUIZ 4

1. Merry
2. A minstrel
3. Black
4. The Bridge Inn
5. The House of the Stewards
6. The Haunted Mountain
7. 42
8. Gorgoroth
9. Lady Éowyn
10. Prince Imrahil

11. The Shire
12. Merry
13. One
14. Oil
15. Two
16. Gandalf
17. Lady Éowyn
18. Quickbeam
19. Gollum
20. Théoden's

21. King Elessar
22. Faramir
23. Four
24. Linhir
25. Beregond

26. Faramir
27. The Lockholes
28. The Paths of the Dead
29. True
30. A green cape

31. Lady Éowyn
32. Gimli
33. Lotho Baggins
34. With bows and arrows
35. Food
36. Gandalf
37. Buckland Gate
38. Beregond
39. Isildur
40. The Third Age

41. Beregond
42. Lebennin
43. Frodo
44. Mr Butterbur
45. Legolas
46. The Anduin
47. Frodo
48. Frodo and Sam
49. Seven thousand
50. Ale

QUIZ 5

1. Gimli
2. March
3. Ecthelion
4. Two
5. A pipe
6. 50 paces
7. Bergil
8. Denethor
9. Frodo
10. Frodo

11. Théoden
12. Aragorn
13. The Houses of Healing
14. The Prancing Pony
15. North
16. Denethor
17. Half the way
18. Frogmorton
19. Ringló Vale
20. Imrahil

21. Bilbo's
22. Faramir
23. Théoden
24. Sam's
25. False

26. Gandalf
27. The date that Sauron fell
28. False
29. Anduin
30. Gimli

31. A healing herb
32. Sam
33. He pardoned them
34. Sixth wall
35. More beautiful
36. Orcs'
37. Gimli
38. Prince Imrahil's
39. True
40. Aragorn

41. Lady Éowyn
42. Pippin
43. Gollum
44. A horn
45. Faramir
46. The enemy
47. Chapter 80
48. Chambers of Fire
49. Pippin
50. Denethor

QUIZ 6

1. Forlong
2. Gandalf
3. Denethor
4. Sauron's Road
5. Sam
6. Sam
7. Arwen
8. Pippin
9. A shirt
10. Dernhelm

11. Saruman
12. Aragorn
13. Red
14. Arwen
15. Woses
16. Seven
17. A knife
18. Shagrat
19. Gondor
20. 50

21. Elrond
22. Isenmouthe
23. True
24. True
25. Faramir
26. Mindolluin

27. Bill Ferny
28. Denethor
29. Aragorn
30. Lady Éowyn

31. A knife wound
32. True
33. True
34. Pippin
35. Precious
36. Hirgon
37. A ladder
38. False
39. Gandalf
40. Thirteen days

41. Fell to his death
42. The Shire
43. Nuncheon
44. An eagle
45. A battering ram
46. Frodo
47. Ten
48. Five
49. A whip
50. The Battle of the Pelennor Fields

QUIZ 7

1. Rohan
2. Gandalf
3. Merry and Pippin
4. Woses
5. Deputy Mayor
6. Sam
7. Gondor
8. Hill-trolls
9. Legolas
10. Three

11. Gorgûn
12. A wall
13. Lady Éowyn
14. River
15. Frodo
16. Less than a week
17. Angry and rude
18. Leechcraft
19. Bag End
20. 25

21. Seven hours
22. One
23. Umbar
24. Pippin
25. His hand
26. Woses
27. Aragorn

28. To stop Frodo from drinking poisoned water
29. True
30. Ingold

31. False
32. Sam
33. True
34. Rammas Echor
35. A tent
36. An eagle
37. Aragorn's
38. A tree
39. 4000
40. Forlong the Fat

41. Gandalf
42. The heads of dead people
43. Dabs
44. Gondor's
45. His hand
46. Lady Éowyn
47. A wolf
48. Merry
49. Six
50. Lady Éowyn